DOLLS

FROM KEWPIE TO BARBIE AND BEYOND

DOLLS

FROM KEWPIE TO BARBIE AND BEYOND

JUDITH EDISON

SMITHMARK

This edition published in 1994
by SMITHMARK Publishers Inc.,
16 East 32nd Street
New York, New York 10016

SMITHMARK books are available
for bulk purchase for sales
promotion and premium use. For
details write or telephone the
Manager of Special Sales,
SMITHMARK Publishers Inc., 16
East 32nd Street, New York, NY
10016. (212) 532-6600.

Produced by Brompton Books
Corp.,
15 Sherwood Place
Greenwich, CT 06830

ISBN 0-8317-2262-2

Printed in Slovenia

10 9 8 7 6 5 4 3 2 1

Page 1: *The joys of childhood and a lifetime companion.*

Pages 2-3: *Barbie's Magical Motor Home.*

Above: *Cabbage Patch Kids were the most successful dolls of the 1980s.*

CONTENTS

Introduction

The history of dolls is as old as the history of mankind itself, and down the centuries they have had many roles: they have been religious artifacts; they have been decorative objects for display rather than play; and, of course, they have been childhood playthings. Equally, dolls have been produced in a bewildering array of materials, from clay and wood through to the most modern plastics, each advance being, to a large extent, determined by the technological sophistication of the particular society in question.

Dolls with religious significance are associated with many ancient civilizations, particularly Greece, Rome, China, and Egypt. Dolls also exist dating from the Dark Ages to the eighteenth century, but are extremely rare. In reality, of the dolls that can be found today, almost all date from the middle of the nineteenth century to the present. Older types are obviously of interest to collectors, while more recent dolls are usually – though not exclusively – objects of play.

The second half of the nineteenth century saw a ballooning of doll manufacture for many reasons, including the emergence of a wealthy middle class with money to spare for nonessential items. The materials used were often fragile, and the dolls were not inexpensive. Consequently, many were objects to be admired rather than given as presents to children. Centers of production were found in Europe, notably in Germany and France, a situation that would remain essentially unchanged until the end of World War I.

Following the Great War, the United States would gradually bloom into the major doll producer. Europe, ravaged by four years of conflict, was, to an extent, in economic ruin, and many traditional companies found it hard to maintain their markets when, clearly, dolls were not an essential purchase. This trend continued into the post-World War II era, fueled by new, durable materials, and cheaper products aimed at the mass market. The impact of the arrival of Mattel's Barbie in the early 1960s cannot be overestimated. Superbly marketed, and supported by an ever-increasing range of accessories, Barbie quickly became the best-selling doll of all time, and spawned a host of imitators.

Left: *An English oak doll from the seventeenth century.*

Below: *An unmarked French fashion doll – possibly by Jumeau – dating from the last quarter of the nineteenth century.*

As was briefly mentioned, dolls have been made in numerous materials. Some have come and gone, others have proved more enduring. Cloth, for example, is one of the oldest materials from which dolls have been made, and is still in use today. Rubber, a substance which initially seemed to offer many possibilities, was soon found to have shortcomings (it deteriorated over time, and paint was prone to flaking). Similarly, Celluloid, a mid-nineteenth-century invention, was popular for a time until it became clear that it was easily damaged and, most worryingly, was highly flammable.

Left: *An early clay doll of the fifth century B.C. from Greece that was probably of religious significance.*

Above: *A Dutch doll from the eighteenth century depicting a stallholder.*

The reasons behind this are fairly straightforward: the growth of marketing aimed at children, and the impact of television in the home. Dolls increasingly – but not exclusively – were being manufactured of characters that would be familiar to children. Media companies were quick to appreciate the potential of this new field, and television series, movies and, in fact, a whole array of consumer products, spawned dolls and their accessories. Indeed, in the recent past, certain television programs have been little more than extended advertisements for the products of a particular company.

Dolls have come a long way from their origins in antiquity, particularly over the last 150 years or so. They are still made from a wide range of materials, and many are produced purely as collectors' items. However, the largest market today – and for the foreseeable future – is for children. Dolls now have the looks to make them attractive, and the durability to survive in the rough world of the nursery. This is their story.

Today, doll manufacturers, for obvious reasons, have to ensure that the materials used in doll-making will not, in the normal course of events, injure children. Vinyl, which became the most important material in the immediate post-1945 world, is both soft and durable, making it an excellent choice for modern manufacturers.

Alongside the development of new materials, there has also been an evolution in the look of dolls. For the first half of the nineteenth century, dolls had the look of stylish women dressed in the clothes of the period. These were not likely to appeal to children – not that that was the manufacturers' intention. By the 1850s, a new style of doll – known as a bébé – was emerging, that had the look of a young girl. These had softer, often more realistic, features that were more likely to appeal to children, though their expressions were a little bland, and the materials from which they were constructed did not make them appropriate gifts for the nursery.

As the nineteenth gave way to the twentieth century, new dolls with much more expressive – and realistic – faces, known as "characters," began to appear. Many of these may still have been aimed at collectors but, clearly, they would also appeal to children. As dolls became more lifelike and potentially more attractive to children, and as more durable materials became available, it was but a small step for manufacturers to aim their product at the nursery rather than the display case. Such trends are discernible in the first half of the twentieth century, but really blossomed after 1945.

Above left: *A baldheaded baby doll manufactured by the British National Doll Company in the first half of the 1930s.*

Right: *Barbie by Mattel is undoubtedly the most popular and successful doll of all time.*

Above: *A doll made by Dean's Rag Book Co. in the 1940s.*

Chapter ONE

The Golden Age

Left: *A selection of dolls, including a pair (at rear) by the German company of Kämmer & Reinhardt, and a winking doll (with cap) by Kestner & Co. Both companies were based in the Thuringian town of Waltershausen.*

Above: *A doll produced by the Russian-born Armand Marseille, who established his factory in the German town of Köppelsdorf in the second half of the nineteenth century.*

For the first 15 years of the twentieth century and, indeed, for the previous 40 years, Germany was the most important doll-manufacturing center in the world. During this long period, German dolls of every type of subject were made in every conceivable material, and produced in huge quantities. It was only the loss of overseas markets in the United States and the rest of Europe during World War I and the economic recession that blighted Germany in the years after the conflict that undermined Germany's pre-eminence in doll-making.

The major manufacturers, companies such as Gebrüder Heubach and Louis Wolf and Co., were mostly established from the 1850s onward and, perhaps remarkably, most were concentrated in Thuringia, an area in the country's southeast. In Thuringia, the focus of the doll-making business were the towns of Waltershausen and Sonneberg, centers which produced dolls in most materials including wood, papier-mâché, bisque and porcelain. The close proximity of the various manufacturers brought many benefits to the individual companies, notably in the areas of new techniques and improved craftsmanship. Indeed, the pre-eminent doll-makers of the region are credited with creating the character baby doll.

One of the most prolific of the Thuringian manufactures was that established by Russian-born Armand Marseille, which was based in Köppelsdorf. His output was both extensive and of high quality, though prices for the dolls were comparatively low. The company was founded in the late nineteenth century when Marseille bought a toy factory from one Mathias Lambert. The company became known as a supplier of bisque heads to the likes of Louis Wolf and Charles Bergmann. Marseille's son, also named Armand, married into the family of doll-maker Ernst Heubach, who had been in business since 1887. The company suffered from the ravages of World War I, but survived in production until the late 1920s.

The most common Marseille doll, one produced in considerable numbers from just after the outbreak of World War I, was known as the A.M. 390. The dolls had jointed bodies with straight, rather stick-like legs. Of the dolls produced before the A.M. 390, the doll based on the mold numbered 370 was perhaps most typical of

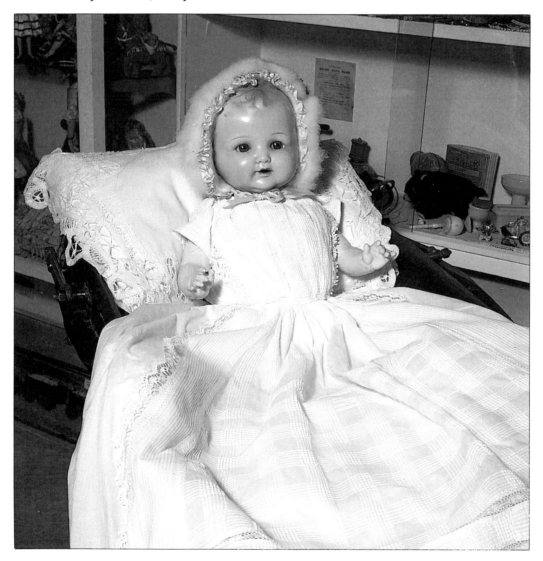

Left: *One of the many fine dolls manufactured by Armand Marseille. This particular example dates from the early 1880s.*

Right: *Marked with the mold number A.M. 370, this Marseille doll dates from before World War I and is one of the company's more commonplace products.*

Far right: *A Kestner character doll. Large ears and chubby arms were a common feature of this German company's designs.*

Marseille's output. It comprised a shoulderplate head sitting atop a fairly basic cloth body with composition arms and rather thick, stuffed legs. The face had an open mouth and somewhat simply drawn eyebrows. Although rather a basic design, when dressed these dolls have an attractive presence.

The most popular of the Marseille dolls are those belonging to the "Dream Babies" series which first appeared in 1924. They were produced in huge quantities and in a variety of sizes. The coloring ranged from a pale bisque to a much ruddier hue. Body materials also varied. For example, larger dolls can be found with stuffed body and composite hands; smaller versions of the "Dream Babies" series often had a five-piece composition body.

Kestner & Co., based in Waltershausen, possibly the only German company of the time to manufacture both the heads and bodies for the dolls, and probably the founder of the industry in Thuringia, began production in the first quarter of the nineteenth century, advertising dolls with papier-mâché heads and leather bodies as early as 1823. The company was founded by Johannes Daniel

Kestner, and was passed on to his grandson Adolph in 1872. In the middle part of the century, Kestner concentrated on producing wax-papier-mâché dolls with china heads, but after his death in 1859 the company expanded by buying into a porcelain factory. Output was then diversified to include both Parian and bisque heads, for which Kestner became renowned. Johannes's grandson Adolph ran the company from 1872 until 1918. In 1930 Kestner merged with Kämmer and Reinhardt.

Kestner & Co. began to make character dolls rather late, around the close of the first decade of the twentieth century. The company produced both the heads and bodies of its dolls, and most consisted of five separate body pieces. Perhaps the best-known character dolls was the 200 series, with the 211 being considered the most popular. It can be recognized by its high-quality bisque, and a head that has either an open mouth with teeth or a mouth with the lips apart but uncut. One of the more unusual products of the Kestner & Co. factory was a four-headed dolls' set. In most cases these were produced with three character heads and a complete body with a young-girl head. Heads could be swapped onto the

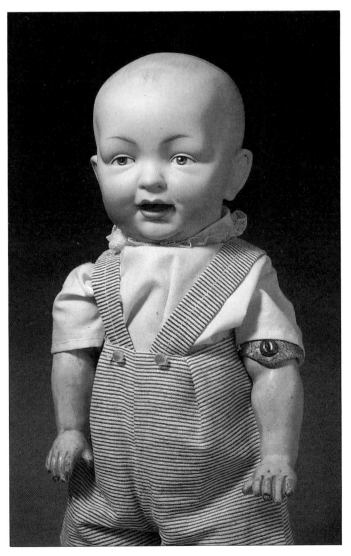

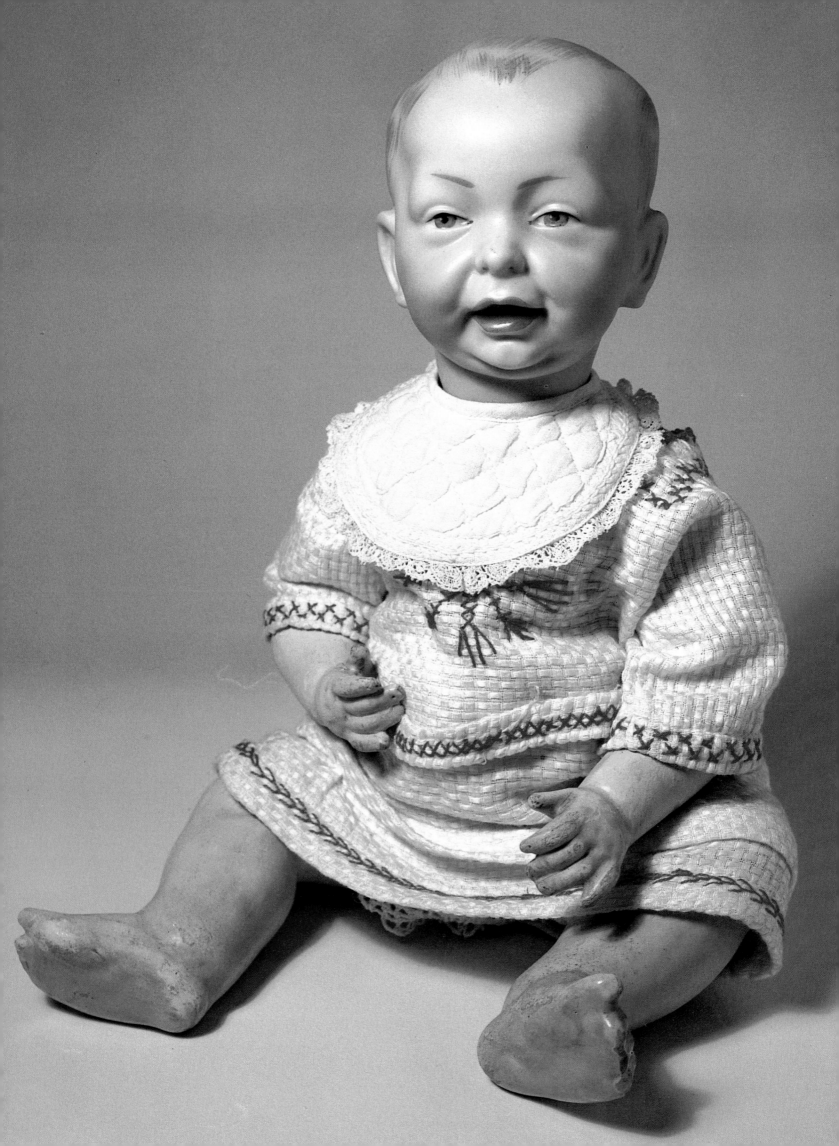

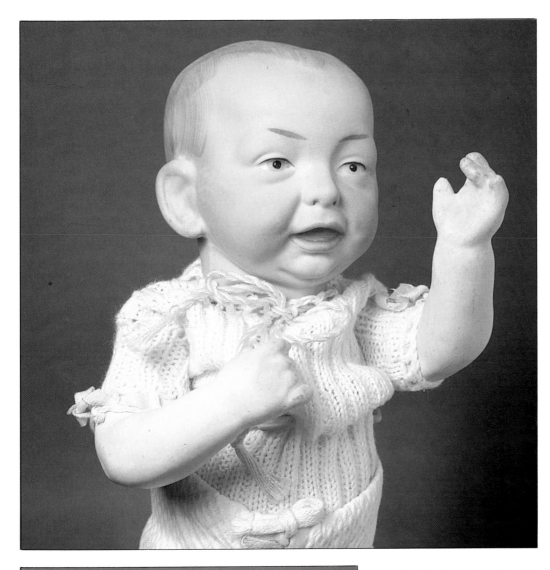

Far left: *A Kämmer & Reinhardt doll based on the famous mold 100, dating from c.1913. Dolls of this type were known as "Kaiser Babies," as they were allegedly modeled on the German emperor's son. Distinctive characteristics include an inwardly bent arm, giving a foreshortened look.*

Left: *A close-up view of a Kämmer & Reinhardt character doll showing the foreshorting effect of the bent arm. Blue eyes were a common feature of the company's dolls.*

Below left: *A highly competent Japanese copy of a Kämmer & Reinhardt doll from 1915.*

socket body and each of the four heads had painted eyes and a closed mouth.

Kämmer & Reinhardt, famed for the production of character dolls of outstanding quality which are now highly valued by collectors, was founded in Waltershausen in the 1880s. Ernst Kämmer was already an expert doll-maker, and is credited with such innovations as a new stringing method for dolls' bodies and cutting out dolls' mouths to insert teeth. Before his death, Kämmer modeled all of the company's dolls; subsequently (from 1902 onward) much of the work was undertaken by the firm of Simon & Halbig. Franz Reinhardt was a dynamic businessman and, after Kämmer's death, purchased the Heinrich Handwerk factory, which was producing ball-jointed bodies and heads. In 1927 Kämmer and Reinhardt also bought the firm of Simon & Halbig which produced heads. By 1932, Reinhardt's expansion plans had borne fruit: the company was undoubtedly the largest manufacturer in Waltershausen.

Kämmer and Reinhardt are said to have led the way in the development of character baby heads after visiting an exhibition by innovative doll designer Marion Kaulitz,

Right: *A superbly realized and beautifully clothed example of the craft of German manufacturers Simon & Halbig, a company based in Thuringia and established in the late 1860s.*

Below right: *The manufacturer's mark on the rear of the head of a doll produced by Simon & Halbig.*

who was based in Munich. Their new product marked a decisive move away from the rather flat, stilted faces of previous dolls, to the more realistic look associated with character dolls. By the early 1900s the new doll types had become so firmly established that the company had difficulty in keeping up with demand. Certainly, character dolls had by this stage become hugely popular. The range of molds produced by the company was large and of genuinely high quality. For example, mold 114, created in 1910 and allegedly based on one of Reinhardt's nephews, was used to produce both boy and girl character heads, known respectively as Hans and Gretchen; the so-called "Kaiser" baby (it was not, in fact, modeled on the German emperor's son but was based on the son of the artist who created the head), mold 116, had molded hair and an open mouth with teeth and a tongue.

Simon & Halbig, based in the town of Grafenhain, concentrated initially on creating dolls' heads in both Parian and papier-mâché, buying in bodies from other manufacturers to complete the work, or selling its heads to

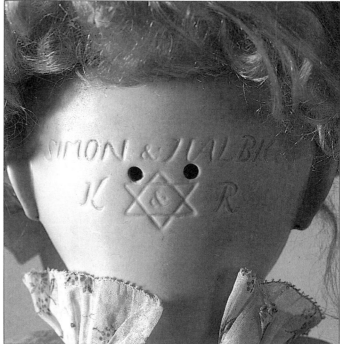

Left: *Simon & Halbig specialized in making dolls with finely detailed oriental features which are much sought after by collectors today. This particular example dates from c.1895.*

others to complete the doll-making process. Among its customers were German firms such as Kämmer & Reinhardt and a number of French concerns. The company made some notable innovations: the use of colored bisque for African-American dolls, and faces with Far Eastern features, as well as Chinese and Native American heads. The Oriental dolls are highly prized. One example dating from the late nineteenth century, cataloged as 1129 Dep. 6, is characterized by an open mouth with visible teeth and almond-shaped glass eyes. The doll was manufactured in golden bisque with a jointed body of wood and composition. Clothing was, of course, suitably exotic.

The company was founded in the mid-nineteenth century, but it was only after 1900 that it began to produce the character heads which became noted for their fine molding and lovely decoration. One of the most famous and collectable of their designs came from mold 1249, known as Santa, which was registered at the turn of the century.

One of the most famous of Germany's doll designers and -makers was Käthe Kruse, who was born in Breslau, Silesia, during 1883. Her design work started when she began making dolls for her very large family – she had seven children. Kruse worked in cloth, being dissatisfied with bisque dolls, which she considered too fragile for the often rough world of children at play. Kruse was an artist by training and her husband a sculptor, and she used her skills to produce very lifelike dolls using her children as inspiration.

The earliest Kruse-designed dolls for the general market were produced by the firm of Kämmer & Reinhardt, but are generally considered to be of poorer quality than those she later made after 1912 in, first, Bad Kösen and, after World War II, in Donauwörth. Kruse died in 1968, but dolls bearing her name are still made today.

To make her dolls, Kruse first sculpted a head and then made a mold from the resulting shape. Stiffened muslin was used to make the actual doll's head and, once shaped, would be sprayed with a fixing solution and then painted. The heads were filled with either absorbent cot-

Right: *An eample of a Käthe Kruse* Träumerchen *("Little Dreamer") doll from the mid-1920s. Characterized by sleeping eyes and a navel, the doll had a body filled with sand.*

Left: *A long-haired Simon & Halbig doll from the end of the nineteenth century.*

Right: *A Käthe Kruse doll dating from the mid-1920s. Kruse began making dolls for her children, and strove to create ones that were capable of bearing up to the often rough world of the nursery.*

Right: *Although Margarete Steiff is credited with creating the German teddy bear, she also manufactured dolls in felt, plush and velvet. Characteristic of her designs is the seaming which runs vertically down the front of the face. This example dates from c.1910.*

Below right: *Another typical doll from the Steiff company, dating from the same period as the previous example. Blue or black button eyes were common on Steiff's fabric dolls.*

ton or deer fur to give them a suitable weight. The dolls' bodies were of cloth which, after suitable preparation, was washable. Kruse's earliest bodies were finely detailed, with navels and wide hips. Her dolls are signed on the bottom of the left foot, where a serial number also appears.

Her first doll, indeed her only design until 1922, appeared in 1911, prosaically known as "Doll I." Later dolls included the *Träumerchen* ("Little Dreamer"), which was marketed in the mid-1920s and featured a navel and sleeping eyes. Perhaps surprisingly, Kruse made only five different heads in the period from 1910 to 1956. Before 1928 Kruse dolls were made with heads sewn onto the bodies; it was not until the following year that heads capable of being turned were produced. Another innovation at this time was the use of real hair; previously, painted hair had dominated the Kruse output.

Although perhaps more famous for its teddy bears, Steiff also produced dolls. The business began in 1877, when Margarete Steiff of the town of Giengen in Württemberg began working with her nephew, Richard, to

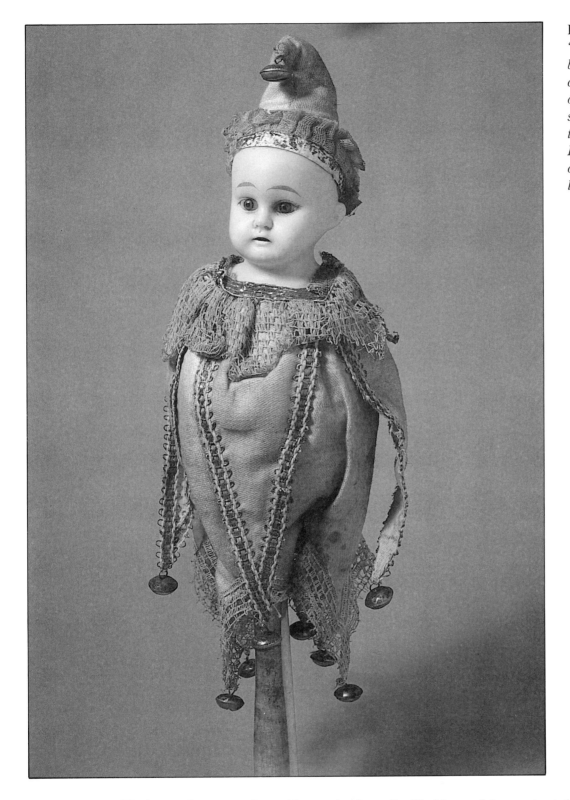

Left: *An Ernst Heubach "marotte" doll from the beginning of the twentieth century. Marottes consisted of a head mounted on a stick, many of which, when twirled, played a tune. Heubach, active until 1930, concentrated on the output of less expensive bisque dolls.*

make felt dolls. Their creations were favorably received, so much so that they were able to move into factory production. Margarete Steiff died in 1909, but the family firm continues to the present.

Most of Margarete Steiff's dolls were made from felt, plush or velvet, with a rather odd-looking seam down the face. In 1904 she began using metal ear buttons which were either plain or embossed with elephants; in the following year the button appeared printed with the name

Steiff. Most of her output falls into the category of character dolls such as "The Butler."

The company of Alt, Beck & Gottschack operated from 1854 until 1930 and was based in Nomendorf in Germany. Although not all of its dolls are marked, some carry the logo A.B.&G. The company made numerous character bisque heads and dolls. In the 1920s it manufactured bisque heads for the popular and famous American "Bye-Lo Babies."

Above: *A selection of piano dolls from the 1850s. As the name suggests, these were ornamental dolls to be displayed rather than for play.*

Right: *A collection of dolls produced by Gebrüder Heubach. Based in Thuringia, this company is best known for its range of character dolls with bisque heads that display a variety of expressions.*

Gebrüder Heubach, based in Lichte, was founded in 1820 to produce porcelain for the manufacture of bisque dolls' heads and figurines, but by 1905 the company had moved over to creating complete dolls. The Heubach brothers became recognized for the variety of their bisque character dolls, but also produced decorative "Piano Babies" (all-bisque figures which came with a variety of often appealing features that were, unsurprisingly, often found displayed on pianos) and figurines for positioning on mantelpieces. The heads of the company's dolls had a variety of expressions and were usually finely modeled. However, poorly made bodies often detracted from the overall quality of the craftsmanship.

Not to be confused with Gebrüder Heubach, is the work of Ernst Heubach, who was active between 1887 and 1930. Based in Köppelsdorf, Thuringia, he concentrated his efforts on producing a range of cheaper dolls, which are not always considered to be of the highest quality, in bisque. Beatrix Heubach, the founder's daughter, wed the son of Armand Marseille, an event that led to the merger of the two production centers under the title *Köppelsdorfer Porzellanfabrik*.

Friedrich Edmund Winkler, who was involved in doll manufacture until 1912, established his business in Sonneberg, Thuringia, in 1882. As was not uncommon at the time, Winkler gathered together the parts for his dolls from a variety of local sources. Although the evidence is patchy, it seems likely that he geared his production to the French market, where he had considerable success: he won the prestigious Medaille d'Or in 1899.

Franz Schmidt, a manufacturer who began producing dolls in the 1890s and continued until 1930, is regarded as

something of an innovator. His company specialized in making both heads (in wood, composition, bisque, Celluloid and rubber, though some Schmidt dolls do have Simon & Halbig heads), and bodies, often ball-jointed. Among his more renowned creations is a doll with pierced nostrils, introduced just before World War I, and he also introduced movable tongues which appeared at roughly the same time.

The United States originally imported most of its dolls for much of the nineteenth century but in the latter part of the century doll manufacturers began to spring up in three main areas: New England, Philadelphia and New York. As a general rule, at least initially, heads were imported from Europe and fixed on home-produced bodies.

Ludwig Greiner, a German doll-maker who emigrated to the United States and set up a factory in Philadelphia, is remembered as the man who received the first patent for a doll's head in the country. The date was March 30, 1858. Greiner concentrated on producing heads made from papier-mâché, or from composition and cloth.

His earliest creations are said to resemble England's Queen Victoria, with molded hair parted down the center. Originally the hair was black, but Greiner went on to produce dolls' heads with blond hair. The bodies for these dolls were often crude, homemade designs of stuffed cloth, but some were made by Jacob Lamann, himself a resident of Philadelphia. These consisted of stuffed cloth with leather arms and legs; a common motif

Far left: *A poured wax doll by the firm of Cuno & Otto Dressel dating from the 1870s. The oldest-known doll manufacturer, the company, originally known simply as Dressel after its founder, was established in 1700.*

Left: *An "Uncle Sam" doll by Cuno & Otto Dressel dating from 1896 and squarely aimed at the American market. The company continued as a doll manufacturer until the end of World War II.*

was red or blue striped socks matched with leather boots in yellow, blue and red.

Perhaps the leading manufacturer of the early part of this century was A. Schoenhut & Co., which was established in Philadelphia. Albert Schoenhut, born in Germany, moved to the United States at the age of 17 and made a name for himself with his Humpty Dumpty Circus, a collection of clown-like figures and animals, along with various items of circus paraphernalia. Characters created by Schoenhut included a ringmaster, lion tamer, female acrobat and circus rider. In 1911 he began manufacturing robust, fully articulated wooden dolls strung with wire, with carved heads and painted or sleeping eyes. The dolls were jointed at the neck, shoulders,

elbows, wrists, hips, knees and ankles, so that they could be posed. His best-known creations are generally referred to as "pouty" characters. Most of Schoenhut's dolls had painted intaglio eyes, though sleeping eyes are also found.

Izannah F. Walker of Central Falls, Rhode Island, who died at the end of the 1880s, is considered the first manufacturer of cloth and rag dolls in the United States. She gained a patent in 1873, though there is evidence to suggest that she was making dolls as early as the 1840s. All of her dolls are considered highly desirable by collectors, particularly those which have bodies made from muslin. Othersof her dolls are covered with stockinet with details picked out in oil paints.

Far left: *A pair of dolls made by English manufacturer Herbert John Meech, who was active from 1865–1917. Meech concentrated on manufacturing poured-wax and composition dolls, and supplied the British royal family.*

Left: *A John Edwards crying doll from the 1870s. Edwards, based in England, was a large-scale manufacturer – by the 1871 London Exhibition, it is thought that the company was producing over 20,000 dolls per week. This rare example of his work shows the fine detail that he achieved in his more expensive creations.*

Below and below left: *Two examples of dolls produced by the Montanari company dating from the second half of the nineteenth century. Though London-based, the firm's founder, Augusta Montanari, was Italian.*

Martha Jenks Chase, who was active in doll-making from the 1880s to the mid-1920s, was based in Pawtucket, Rhode Island, and was responsible for the manufacture of stockinet dolls, with the material stretched over the limbs and a face mask. Faces were detailed in oil-based paints, with the hair painted in rough strokes. Prior to 1920 the bodies were jointed at the shoulder, hips, knees and elbows; later dolls were jointed at the shoulders and hips only. Chase also produced a range of cloth dolls of well-known characters, including those from Lewis Carroll's ever-popular *Alice in Wonderland*. Her success led to the foundation of the Chase Stockinette Doll Co.

The Arnold Print Works, active until 1925, was based in North Adenes, Massachusetts, and concentrated on manufacturing unusual do-it-yourself, cutout dolls in printed fabrics. In fact, many of the dolls were used in advertising, promoting such well-known brand names as Kelloggs, while others were inspired by characters from comics, such as Little Orphan Annie. Another manufacturer of fabric dolls was Art Fabric Mill of New York, which was active until 1910 and, unusually, manufactured African-American fabric dolls.

Grace Storey Putnam, originally of Oakland, California, had a career as an art-college teacher, but made her name as a designer of dolls' heads and as the creator of the famous "Bye-Lo Baby" for the Borgfeldt doll company. The Bye-Lo doll had the face of a very young baby and came in a variety of materials – bisque, wax and composition. Heads were made in Germany by George Borgfeldt, among other companies.

As in America, the home-grown doll-producing sector in England was given a boost by the ban on German imports which occurred during World War I. Initially, many of the dolls, made from a wide range of materials, were rather crudely executed.

The Diamond Pottery Co. Ltd. of Stoke-on-Trent in the English Midlands was an offshoot of a porcelain company, and produced many generally inferior-quality china-headed dolls with a generally low quality of painted finish. A firm operating in Staffordshire, the Doll Pottery Co., was in production from 1915 to 1922 and manufactured an enormous range of dolls and dolls' heads in a wide variety of sizes and formats. Other manufacturers treading a similar path were W. H. Goss and Co., which ceased production in 1944, and Hancock & Sons, which departed the field in 1937. None of their output was that remarkable, but Hancock & Sons did have a large number of head styles – open-mouthed, molded hair and so on.

If the output of porcelain dolls in England in the first part of the twentieth century was generally unremarkable, certain manufactures of fabric dolls are considered more collectable, particularly the so-called "bou-

doir" dolls of companys such as Chad Valley and Dean's Rag Book Co.

Chad Valley Co. Ltd., a company founded in Birmingham in 1823, focused production on promotional dolls of popular characters. In the 1920s, for example, it created Mabel Lucy Atwell Dolls and a range based on the *Snow White and the Seven Dwarfs* fairy tale. Among the materials employed in manufacture were stockinet, velvet and felt. Felt was frequently used. Originally based on beaver or rabbit fur, and later wool, the advantage being the ease with which it could be steam-molded into the required shape.

Dean's Rag Book Co. Ltd, a subsidiary of Bean & Sons Ltd. of London, was established in 1903. Its first dolls were printed on cloth, to be made up at home by the purchaser; by 1920, however, the company had moved into the production of molded felt dolls. The Evripose range of felt dolls, initiated in 1923, had printed shoes and socks, features that became a hallmark of the company. Dean's also produced dolls of favorite children's characters such as Charlie Chaplin, Alice in Wonderland and Mother Goose.

Of all the doll types produced by English manufacturers in the first decades of the twentieth century, the most highly regarded were those sculpted in wax. Among the many companies engaged in this type of work were Charles and William Marsh and Lucy Peck. The Marshes, working until just before World War I, pro-

Left: *Albert Schoenhut, president of the A. Schoenhut company of Philadelphia, was born in Germany but emigrated at the age of 17. From 1911, his company started to make jointed dolls with wooden bodies.*

Right: *A Lucy Peck doll of Princess Louise as a bride, c.1887. Peck worked from "The Doll's Home" in London, and gained a name for her poured-wax dolls.*

Below: *A Charles Pierotti model of English military hero Lord Roberts, from 1901. Pierotti, London-based but of Italian extraction, concentrated on dolls of high quality for the more expensive end of the market.*

duced both wax and wax-coated papier-mâché forms.

If Germany dominated doll manufacturing from the latter part of the nineteenth century until World War I, it was the French who were famed for the quality and variety of their output in the earlier part of the nineteenth century. Bébés, a word used to describe a jointed girl doll produced by Pierre François Jumeau, originated in the 1850s.

From the 1860s until the 1890s, France succeeded Germany as the world's premier doll-producing country, albeit focusing on high-quality dolls for the children of the burgeoning industrial middle class. However, as the German firms moved into creating dolls for the top end of the market, the French were forced onto the defensive. In 1899, in a move which in some way acknowledged the pre-eminence of their German rivals, the French formed the Société Française de Fabrication de Bébés et Jouets (S.F.B.J.).

The S.F.B.J., which carried on until after World War II, concentrated on making bébés, character and colored dolls, and babies. Perhaps the best examples of the society's work were its character dolls, which first appeared a few years before the outbreak of World War I. Generally, they are of a higher quality than much of the S.F.B.J.'s output and are found with a variety of ex-

Far left: *A doll manufactured by the French Société Française de Fabrication de Bébés et Jouets (S.F.B.J.) in 1925.*

Left: *A so-called "long-faced" doll made by the firm of Jumeau, one of the biggest companies of the second half of the nineteenth century.*

Below: *Another example of a Jumeau long-faced doll, originally known as a "Jumeau Triste." These dolls are so named because of their rather sad expressions.*

Below left: *A delightful S.F.B.J. character doll from the beginning of the twentieth century. This particular example has a bisque head atop a jointed composition-and-wood body.*

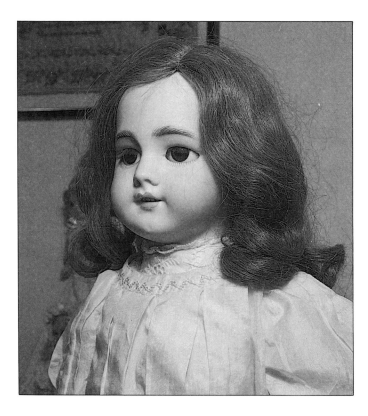

pressions. However, despite the S.F.B.J.'s attempt to protect the French industry from German competition, the association did make extensive use of heads manufactured by its European neighbor, particularly before the outbreak of World War I.

Before the establishment of the S.F.B.J., however, there were a number of famed French manufacturers, chief among these being Jumeau. To give some indication of the importance of this company, in 1881 it produced over 80,000 dolls and in 1889 was employing 1000 workers. In the mid-1870s Emile, the youngest son of the founder, Pierre, took charge of the company and won many awards for the quality of his creations, including a Medaille d'Or at the 1878 Paris Exposition Universelle and a Diplôme d'Honneur from Belgium in 1885. In the 1890s, considered to be the company's finest period, open-mouthed dolls were the most expensive of Jumeau's products.

Jumeau is perhaps best remembered for his pioneering work with dolls known as bébés, idealized representations of a young girl. These designs often had bisque heads topped by real hair or mohair atop a jointed body that had distinctively chubby limbs.

Unfortunately, after Jumeau became subsumed within the structure of S.F.B.J. in 1899, the overall quality of its output declined. Cheaper, German-manufactured heads were imported, and many had rather crudely wrought features and details.

One of Jumeau's greatest French rivals was the company founded in 1866 by Leon Casimir Bru in the Rue St. Denis in Paris, Bru Jeune et Cie. Bru Jeune never com-

peted with Jumeau in terms of quantity, focusing rather on high quality matched to innovative design work. In 1879, for example, the firm introduced the "Bru Teteur" baby doll which could draw liquid into its mouth thanks to a rubber device fitted in its head.

The fortune of Bru Jeune declined somewhat in the final 20 years or so of the nineteenth century. Leon Bru had sold his interest in the company to Henri Celestin Chevrot in 1883, who later in turn passed the company on to Paul Eugène Girard. Initially, Chevrot continued the Bru Jeune tradition of producing high-quality dolls, but with increasing pressure from cheaper German imports, began a move into the lower end of the market, a development that continued during Girard's period of ownership.

Nevertheless, innovations and new designs continued: Girard introduced a talking bébé and a doll that blew kisses. As with many French manufacturers, Bru

Above, far left: *A Jumeau doll from the 1870s. The company was one of the great innovators in the business, and the company's dolls remain highly collectable.*

Above left: *Bru Jeune & Cie, the French firm founded in the 1860s and active until the end of the century, gained a reputation for its bisque-headed bébés and fashion dolls.*

Jeune joined the S.F.B.J. in 1899 and carried on as a doll-maker until the late 1950s, when the then owner, André Girard, sold the company's entire collection.

Another of the outstanding French doll-makers was Jules Nicholas Steiner, originally a Parisian clock manu-facturer who had a factory in the capital from the 1870s until the turn of the century. Given his mechanical back-ground, it is hardly surprising that Steiner became known for mechanical dolls. These include such items as a baby which could both kick and cry. The company's heyday was the decade from 1880 and 1890; in 1889 Steiner was awarded a gold medal at the Paris Exposition Universelle.

The Steiner company, however, went through many changes after the glory days of the 1880s. In 1890 Amadé Lafosse took over the company, although Steiner himself was still involved. The firm was subsequently owned by Lafosse's widow (until 1902), Julie Mettis, who lasted

Above left: *A Bru Jeune & Cie doll dating from the latter part of the nineteenth century. By this time the company had become known as Bru Jeune.*

Above: *A bisque-headed doll of the 1880s, manufactured by the French company Jules Steiner which was active from 1855.*

Right: *A Steiner walking doll from 1885. Jules Steiner had a background as a clockmaker, and many of his dolls were able to walk or talk.*

Far right, center: *This French fashion doll was produced by the firm Gauthier in c.1870; shortly afterward the firm changed its name to Gaultier and gained a high reputation for its top-quality fashion dolls and bébés.*

Far right: *The French company of Schmitt et Fils was Paris-based and active in the second half of the nineteenth century, gaining praise for their its bisque bébés.*

Below, far right: *This doll by Rabery & Delphieu, one of the founders of France's S.F.B.J., from the 1880s is typical of the company's high-quality product.*

until 1903, and then Edmond Daspres, who stayed with Steiner until its closure in 1908. It is widely considered that its dolls from this later period are generally inferior to their earlier cousins.

Gaultier Frères was active from the 1860s until the turn of the century, and concentrated on the production of all-bisque and fashion dolls as well as bébés. François Gaultier, the founder, won a silver medal at the 1878 Paris Exposition Universelle. In 1882 the company underwent a name change to Gaultier et Fils Aine after François's eldest son – Eugène – became a company director; three years later Eugène took charge and the company was rechristened to give it the title by which it is commonly known: Gaultier Frères.

Aside from manufacturing complete dolls, Gaultier Frères also supplied dolls' heads to other manufacturers, notably Rabery & Delphieu. However, the rise of the firm, as was the case with many other French manufacturers, was halted by the tide of German imports in

the late nineteenth century. Gaultier Frères joined the S.F.B.J. in 1899, renting its factory out to the new conglomerate, but, as was common with this development, the overall standard of its output then declined. The Gaultier name contined to appear on dolls until it was dispensed with at the end of World War I.

While the above-mentioned firms dominated French doll manufacture in the late nineteenth and early twentieth centuries, other, smaller, companies also produced a variety of dolls. Danel & Cie was founded in 1889 after Danel had a somewhat acrimonious separation from his former employer, Jumeau. Indeed, Jumeau successfully pursued a lawsuit against Danel on the basis that the latter removed molds and tools from his premises, and enticed key workers away.

Rabery & Delphieu was established in 1856 after Jean Delphieu was granted a license to produce dolls. The company, which again became part of the S.F.B.J. in 1899, bought in heads from Gaultier Frères and placed

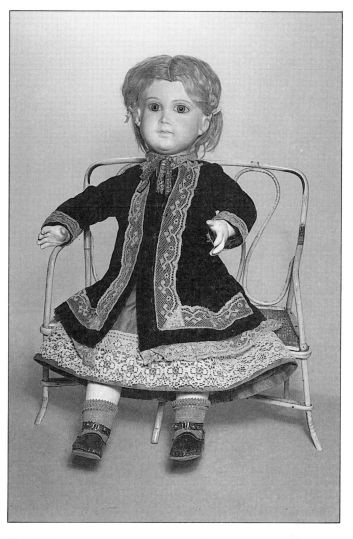

them on bodies made from pink-and-white kid. Innovations were produced, including talking dolls, which first reached the market in the late nineteenth century.

The factory owned by Schmitt et Fils at Nogent-sur-Marne, a company which operated from the 1860s until 1891, concentrated on making bébé and dolls' heads from bisque, porcelain or composition covered with wax. For the 13 years from 1879 until 1891, Schmitt et Fils also advertised an allegedly indestructible "Bébé Schmitt," which featured an eight-ball-jointed body and extra-long, small feet.

The French firm of Gesland Co. did not, in fact, manufacture dolls, but rather assembled the creations of other companies or made parts for them. It operated from the 1860s to the second year of World War I. To cash in on the demand for souvenirs from the wealthier middle classes who had undertaken a tour of Europe, the Gesland Co. often married bodies dressed in regional costumes to heads from Gaultier.

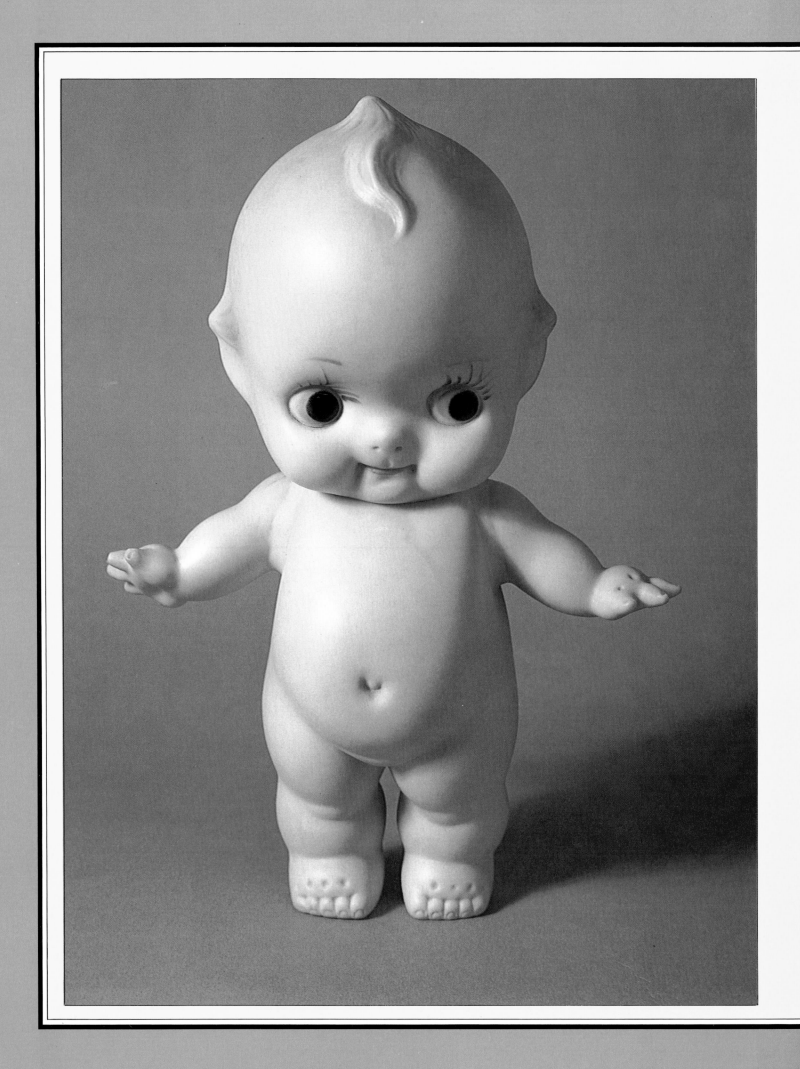

CHAPTER TWO

New Directions

Left: *The world-famous Kewpie was created by American illustrator Rose O'Neill, and the first examples appeared in 1913. Design work on the doll was carried out by Joseph Kallus, who was supervised by O'Neill.*

Above: *A bisque Googly doll manufactured in the 1920s. American illustrator Grace Gebbie Drayton is regarded as the creator of these round-eyed, impish figures.*

As was discussed in the previous chapter, the effects of World War I on doll-making were profound. Germany, for several decades the leading manufacturer and exporter, lost its dominant position. Between 1914 and 1918, the country's trading links with the likes of France, England and the United States were obviously severed and, as a defeated nation with an economy in ruins, Germany was in no fit state to regain its pre-eminence in the interwar period. In response to the wartime and postwar shortages of dolls, many new manufacturers sprang up in the aforementioned countries, particularly in the United States.

A second distinctive strand in the history of dolls that is evident in the years following World War I was the move away from traditional doll "types." Previously, dolls had a very traditional, formal look to them, almost as if they were for show, which in many cases they were. After 1918, the look of dolls, as well as the material available, changed and diversified. Quite simply, they began to be aimed much more at children. Characters from comics, cartoons and fairy tales, all of which would be familiar to and popular with the younger generation,

were often used as the inspiration for new dolls. Completely new designs also had a look and robustness which would find success with the younger ages.

In the United States, many of the new companies were based in New York, and many of them produced what are known as composition dolls, though all types of materials were used. In fact, doll-makers in the United States outstripped their German rivals in the production of composition dolls for virtually the whole of the interwar period. Composition was a cheap alternative to more expensive material such as bisque and porcelain. Its major ingredient consisted of wood or paper pulp, bound together with materials such as rags, bones and eggs. The major drawbacks with composition were that it was prone to crazing and flaking, was susceptible to water damage, and could not be easily cleaned. As we shall see, the shortcomings of composition as the basis of doll manufacture would lead to the development of new and more durable materials.

Although there were many famous doll-making companies in the United States, it is perhaps best to look at the creators of two of the most popular doll types of all

Far left: *Rose O'Neill (in the wide-brimmed hat), the creator of the Kewpie doll, meets some of her young admirers.*

Left: *A German example of an O'Neill Kewpie. Although New York's George Borgfeldt & Co. held the doll's manufacturing and distribution rights, demand made it necessary to allow other firms to manufacture Kewpies under license.*

Below: *Another Borgfeldt doll was the "Bye-Lo Baby," created by American designer Grace Storey Putnam. It became so popular that it was also known as the "Million-Dollar Baby."*

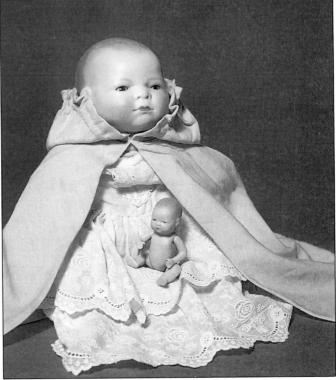

time: Grace Gebbie Drayton, who was one of those credited with developing the character figures known as "Googlies," and Rose O'Neill, an illustrator who devised the characters which would become world-famous – "Kewpies."

Rose O'Neill, who was actively involved in doll design for the first 30 years or so of this century, was an illustrator by trade who created Cupidlike figures to illustrate stories that first appeared in the *Ladies Home Journal* in 1909. Here, charming, mischievous-looking "Kewpies" were supposed to be children's guardian angels. The dolls themselves were actually designed by Joseph Kallus, president of the Cameo Doll Company, though under the watchful eye of O'Neill. Manufacture began in 1913 at the Kestner factory, where the first Kewpies were produced in bisque.

The bisque Kewpies had certain very recognizable features: tiny eyebrows, a virtually bald head with a pointed patch of painted blond hair, sideways-glancing eyes, a tiny snub nose, outstretched hands with splayed fingers, and a very pronounced potbelly. The first Kewpies were an immediate hit, and the Kestner factory

Right: *Italian manufacturers Lenci, based in Turin, gained a reputation for producing high-quality dolls – usually dressed in good-looking clothes – that were more for display than play.*

Far right: *Raggedy Ann, the brainchild of John Gruelle in the early part of the twentieth century, is still produced today. As the name suggests, the dolls are made of rags.*

Below right: *Another example of a Bye-Lo Baby from the 1920s.*

benefited from a huge increase in orders. Demand, however, continued to outstrip supply, and a series of factories, both in Germany and the United States, began to produce the dolls. Licenses to make O'Neill's design were issued by George Borgfeldt & Co., which had a monopoly on the right to manufacture and distribute Kewpies.

Borgfeldt was a New York-based company that had been initially established to import and then distribute high-quality dolls from leading German and French makers throughout the United States. However, designs such as the Kewpie were also commissioned, after which the company farmed out the manufacture to other firms. Another of the company's successful commissions was Grace Storey Putnam's "Bye-Lo Baby" doll, which became one of the most successful creations of all time. The doll was an instant hit with the general public and sales were so great that it was rechristened the "Million-Dollar Baby."

Putnam, one of the finest designers of her generation,

went to inordinate lengths to find a model for her doll, allegedly scouring hospitals and orphanages to find a suitable subject. The doll was manufactured using several different materials: bisque for the head, Celluloid for the hands, and fabric for the body. Several sizes were made available, and some were produced with Celluloid heads.

Although the original dolls were made in bisque (these remain the most prized by today's collectors), the material was not strong enough to take the wear and tear of the nursery, and other materials were therefore introduced, including Celluloid, rubber, fabric, and composition. Generally, the dolls range in height from 2½ inches to about 17 inches, and are found either with or without some type of costume.

In many ways "Googlies," the dolls that were the brainchild of Grace Gebbie Drayton, were similar to O'Neill's Kewpies. They had an equally impish grin, the eyes stared sideways and were topped with short, arching eyebrows, and a small nose. Drayton was an illustrator, and was responsible for the "Campbell Kids" dolls. Googly dolls with bisque heads first arrived in 1911, and for the next two decades and more were produced by a large number of prestigious German companies such as Armand Marseille and Gebrüder Heubach.

Many variations of the basic design were produced by these manufacturers and one of the most popular of the

Far left: *A typical Lenci doll from c.1925 displaying the elaborate costumes that were one of the hallmarks of the company's product.*

Left: *A pair of Norah Wellings dolls. Wellings, a prolific English designer, devised these examples to represent women serving in the Royal Navy and Royal Air Force.*

Below left: *A trio of Lenci dolls portraying a variety of sports, including croquet (left) and golf (right).*

early period came from a mold held by the Kestner company. Mold 221 was used to produce bisque heads of the highest quality which were fitted to a wood-and-composition jointed body. Other companies also produced variations on the original theme. For example, Armand Marseille in the early 1920s produced a Googly-type doll which had a similar wide-eyed look to the original doll but lacked its distinctive smile. It is generally considered to be an inferior version of the original.

Manufacturers in the United States also produced dolls that, if not exact copies of the original Googlies, were very similar. Leon Rees, for example, designed a series of dolls that were marketed under the collective title of "Hug-me-Kiddies." These enjoyed widespread popularity, partly because they were comparatively inexpensive, and partly because they had a very attractive look. Rees's dolls had composition heads featuring eyes

that could be moved by working a lever, and they came in a variety of costumes for both boys and girls. The bodies were made from pink felt.

Rag had been established as a popular medium for doll manufacture long before the twentieth century and remains popular to this day. Although prone to damage due to the rigors of children's play, it had other advantages. A reasonably skilled individual could produce a rag doll cheaply at home with little difficulty; commercially produced rag dolls were generally cheaper than those manufactured from more expensive materials. Indeed, rag dolls tended to be replaced on a regular basis after they had been damaged.

Perhaps the most famous rag dolls created in the United States, and characters that are still produced today, are "Raggedy Ann" and "Raggedy Andy." The dolls were the brainchild of John Gruelle, an artist who

wrote a story about a doll that his daughter Marcella had uncovered in her grandmother's attic. The story was eventually published by P. F. Volland & Company, which was then inundated with requests to produce a doll – Raggedy Ann – based on Gruelle's story.

Initially, Volland put together a batch of 200 dolls which had painted faces and wooden hearts. These proved so successful that the company went over to full-scale commercial production at the end of World War I. "Raggedy Andy," a companion doll to the first creation, followed two years later, and a short time after that a second design of each doll was introduced, having four instead of the original six eyelashes. Rather than being hand-painted, as was the original case, these facial features of the new generation of dolls were printed.

The dolls were subsequently manufactured by a number of different firms from the 1930s onward. The Mollye Goldman Outfitters company, active from 1935 to 1938, produced dolls which featured red hair and only three eyelashes; the Exposition Toy & Doll Company came out with dolls with unusual red noses outlined in black; and the American Novelty Manufacturing Company produced dolls with plain legs at the close of the 1930s.

One of the companies most closely associated with the Raggedy Ann and Raggedy Andy dolls was the Averill Manufacturing Company. The firm, which both designed and made dolls, was founded in 1915 by Rudolf Hopf, Georgene Averill – his sister – and Paul Averill. Aside from the Gruelle-inspired dolls, Averill also produced character dolls, especially cowboy and Native American subjects, as well as a Grace Gebbie Drayton-designed walking "Mama Doll."

Early Averill Raggedy Ann and Andy dolls featured printed faces with shoe-button eyes, a thin black mouth

Top left: *"Flossie Flirt" was marketed by the New York-based Ideal Toy & Novelty Co. Dating from 1925, this doll has a cloth body.*

Top right: *Ideal Novelty Co.'s Shirley Temple doll proved successful thanks to the star's success.*

Above: *An English doll of the 1930s created by Norah Wellings.*

Above right: *The Dionne Quins dolls were based on actual children born in Canada in 1934, and were produced by the Madame Alexander Doll Company.*

that was little more than a fine line broken by a tiny central red spot to indicate the lips, and a distinctive triangular red nose. The dolls' hair was of red wool. The dolls' legs often comprised red-and-white horizontally striped lines. Averill, trading as the Georgene Novelty Company when the first Gruelle-inspired dolls were produced, was still making its earlier range of Raggedy Ann and Andy dolls well into the 1960s.

The success of the Raggedy Ann and Andy dolls led to the creation of other, similar dolls in the 1920s and after. Among these were characters known as "Beloved Belindy," "Percy Policeman," and "Brown Bear."

While, in some ways, the United States was the leading manufacturer of cloth dolls during the interwar period, other countries were also working in the field. One of the major European companies was that of Lenci,

which was founded in 1918. Lenci was the trademark of the firm established by the Italian Enrico di Scavini; the title was di Scavini's name for his wife Elena. In fact, it was Elena who can lay some claim to setting up the company. In 1915, while Enrico was on active service, she began, with her brother, to make dolls in their Turin apartment. The first doll she produced was called "Lencina." Unlike many of the dolls emanating from the United States, Lenci's products were firmly geared toward the more costly end of the market.

These dolls were predominantly made from molded felt and featured jointed bodies. The costumes worn by the dolls were highly detailed and often very brightly colored, patchwork being something of a leitmotif. Lenci was extremely prolific both in the number of dolls produced and the variety of ranges available. Initially, Elena

herself did much of the company's design work but, as it expanded, commissions were given to a number of outside artists. The heyday of Lenci is considered to date from the 1920s (dolls first appeared under the Lenci name in 1922) to the 1940s and, during this period, they had certain clearly identifiable characteristics.

Aside from the colorful clothing and felt construction, the dolls had very expressive faces, usually with painted eyes and eyebrows, though glass eyes are sometimes seen. Features commonly found on Lenci dolls also include zigzag stitching down the back of the neck and, unusually, two fingers of the hand stitched together, though this is by no means always the case with dolls produced by this company.

In England, one of the most renowned producers of fabric dolls was Norah Wellings, who began her career working for the Chad Valley Company before setting up on her own, with her brother Leonard, in 1926. She was based in Wellington in the county of Shropshire, and produced an enormous range of dolls that were available in all price ranges. Some were souvenir dolls that individuals might buy to commemorate a holiday or event.

One of the dolls produced in this category by Wellings

was a sailor character which was often sold on board ships as a keepsake to remind the purchaser of the journey. One of Wellings' earliest commissions in this field was to produce a sailor doll for the Cunard shipping line. Others of her dolls were more conventional, often with a pressed felt face on top of a felt body; facial details were painted onto the fabric.

Wellings also played her part in World War II. During the conflict she created a number of dolls in wartime costume after she had been given the title of "Doll-maker to the British Commonwealth of Nations." Characters to appear included a paratrooper known as "Harry the Hawk," and a pair of female dolls dressed as members of the Royal Air Force and the Royal Navy. In the case of the paratrooper doll, a part of the sales revenue was given to a Royal Air Force charity fund.

The interwar period, with all of its economic problems brought about by the need for reconstruction after World War I, reinforced the trend away from the very high-cost dolls of the early part of the century, and manufacturers attempted to capture a bigger share of the doll-buying market with less "old-fashioned" designs. Traditional doll types were still being produced, but new ranges were also being introduced. These might have been based on characters familiar to children from stories, but they were also increasingly coming from the movies and, a new development, from the world of advertising.

Possibly one of the most widely sold dolls of the period was one based on the character created by the child movie star, Shirley Temple. The doll was originally pro-duced in the United States by the Ideal Novelty & Toy Company of Brooklyn, New York, in 1934. A variety of sizes (and, therefore, prices) was made available, and the sales of the doll were enormous. Originally, the doll consisted of a jointed composition body with brown glass eyes, an open mouth and blonde curly hair.

The Ideal Novelty & Toy Company was founded in the first decade of the twentieth century by Morris Michtom, who gained a reputation as a manufacturer of teddy bears. Michtom branched out into the doll-making world in 1909 with the creation of a composition character doll. Aside from the Shirley Temple doll, Ideal produced other movie-type characters, including the evergreen Snow White and the Seven Dwarfs, Pinocchio, Judy Garland, and Deanna Durbin.

The Snow White doll was produced in two versions: one had a composition head and body, while the second was made of cloth. The dress comprised a red bodice and cape and a voluminous off-white skirt that had the title "Snow White and the Seven Dwarfs" printed on the front, along with the dwarfs, which were individually named along the bottom. One of the problems with movie-star "portrait" dolls, of course, is that of popularity. Some cartoon characters, if they remain popular, do tend to have a much longer life as character dolls.

For manufacturers, this type of doll can have marketing problems. When a star is in his or her heyday, the dolls do very well; when they become less popular so do the dolls. Shirley Temple dolls sold in huge numbers up to the beginning of World War II but then lost out to

Above left: American manufacturer Edward Imeson Horsman is shown here presenting a pair of twin dolls to movie star Edna Murphy in 1924. He produced the popular "Campbell Kids" and "Can't Break 'Em" dolls.

Far left: EFFanBEE, an American-based company, was founded in 1913 by Hugo Baum and Bernard Fleischaker. This doll from 1925 was known as "Bubbles."

Left: A quartet of Shirley Temple dolls dressed in a variety of costumes.

Right: *One of the "Campbell Kid" dolls created by Grace Gebbie Drayton for the famous soup company. Originally produced to advertise a company's product, these types of doll often became popular in their own right.*

Far right, center: *This doll, known as "Margie," was produced by Joseph Kallus's New York-based Cameo Doll Co.*

Far right, below: *"Patsy" was produced by EFFanBEE in 1928. The company gained a reputation for producing hard-wearing dolls that were ideally suited to the world of the nursery.*

Far right: *"Sunny Jim" appeared in England in the 1920s as part of an advertising campaign by an American company to promote a new breakfast cereal called Force.*

newer designs. A revival of Shirley Temple movies in the 1950s led to a brief re-emergence for the dolls, but in hard plastic and vinyl.

Some dolls were also created to cash in on a sudden, and often shortlived, event. For example, the famous Madame Alexander Doll Company of the United States produced a set of five dolls that was known as the Dionne Quins. The real quins – Yvonne, Marie, Emelie, Cecile and Annette – were born in Ontario, Canada, during 1934, and became instant celebrities because of the comparative rarity of multiple births.

Madame Alexander gained sole rights to market the Dionne quintuplets and produced a set of five composi-

tion dolls that had molded hair and sideways-pointing eyes. Dress consisted of flowing nightdresses, bibs (with each one having one of the Dionne babies' names embroidered on it), and cardigans. To complete the set, the company also provided a bed on which the bent-limbed dolls could be posed.

The EFFanBEE Toy Company, an American firm, was founded by Bernard Fleischaker and Hugo Baum, and was registered in 1910. From the early 1920s EFFanBEE established a name producing walking and talking dolls with names such as "Rosemary," "Lovums," "Baby Grumpy" and "New Born Baby." EFFanBEE, the name taken from the first letters of the founders' surnames,

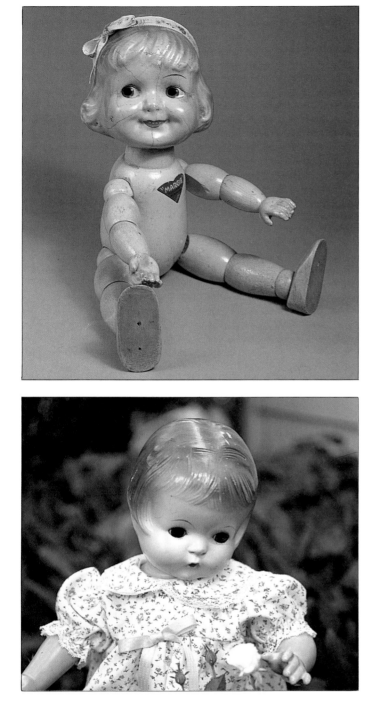

followed Ideal into the world of movie-star and comic-strip portrait dolls.

One such doll was based on the comic character "Skippy," created by cartoonist Percy Crosby. A later movie of the cartoon starred Jackie Cooper, after which Skippy was known as the Jackie Cooper doll. The dolls are characterized by sideways-looking eyes, and faces with chubby cheeks and a small snub nose. EFFanBEE also produced one-off dolls that were based on characters from other areas of popular entertainment, including ventriloquist's dummies. One of the more famous was based on a character which originated with Edgar Bergen in 1930 – Charlie McCarthy, a very well-to-do gentleman who sported evening dress and a monocle. Heads were of composition placed on bodies of stuffed material.

The Cameo Doll Company, presided over by Joseph Kallus, operated from the early 1920s to the first years of the following decade, was based in New York, and concentrated on producing wood-and-composition dolls. Again, the company went along with the new trends in doll characters. One of its most popular designs was a representation of the famous Betty Boop cartoon character, which consisted of a multi-jointed wooden body, usually dressed in a bathing suit, finished off with a composition swivel head that featured molded hair and painted features.

Right: *An English rubber doll of the 1920s. Although rubber was a tough material, it was prone to flaking, as can be seen in this example.*

Far right: *An example of a rubber doll produced by the American Goodyear Company. Dolls of this type were used by the firm to advertise its new type of rubber.*

The Cameo Doll Company did not, however, neglect the more traditional doll types. One of its more successful lines was a series of dolls known as "Scootles." The original work was undertaken by Rose O'Neill, and the company produced a series of dolls that were constructed from bisque and fabric composition. They were produced in a wide range of sizes, to appeal to the pockets of a variety of customers, and also came as African-Americans and Caucasian. Molded hair and jointed bodies were standard.

Dolls initially produced to advertise a particular product also grew in popularity during this period. There are many examples available, but it is worthwhile highlighting just a handful. Perhaps the most famous were the dolls known as the "Campbell Kids," produced for the Campbell Soup Company.

These were designed by Grace Gebbie Drayton and were originally produced by E. I. Horsman in 1910. Later versions were produced by the Aetna Doll & Toy Com-

pany and the American Character Doll Company. Aetna, another New York-based firm, was a producer of dolls, dolls' heads and teddy bears, and was founded in 1909. Its product was originally marketed by George Borgfeldt & Company, and later by Horsman. In 1919, the association was recognized when the two companies merged. The American Character Doll Company, which flourished in the 1920s, concentrated on making character dolls which were sold under the trademark of "Petite."

Edward Imeson Horsman began as a toy distributor but turned to doll manufacture in the first decade of the twentieth century. The company's dolls were made from rag cloth, composition and bisque, and, aside from the Campbell Kids, also produced the so-called "Can't Break 'Em" dolls.

The latter doll was designed by Helen Trowbridge and produced by Horsman from 1911. Again, it was a form of advertisement: in this case to publicize the "Little Fairy Soap" produced by the N. K. Fairbanks Company. The

which the product being sold was known. Hence, the Bisto Kids would not, in all probability, have sold well in the United States, for example. There were, however, dolls made to help spearhead a new marketing campaign for a product previously unknown in a particular region or country. One example from the 1920s was a rather strange-looking character cloth doll known as "Sunny Jim," who could be purchased once a certain number of packet tops had been saved. He was introduced into England from the United States to promote a new product known as Force, a breakfast cereal consisting of malted and toasted wheat flakes.

Sunny Jim looked happy, supposedly because he had been eating Force (the doll was in fact modeled holding a carton of the cereal). Conversely, a second character, known as "Jim Dumps," was modeled with an unhappy expression; quite literally, he was "down-in-the-dumps" because he had not eaten Force first thing in the morning. The campaign was not considered wholly successful, though the character of Sunny Jim continued until World War II and was briefly revived in the 1950s. Interestingly, he was never on offer in the United States.

Some companies also used dolls to advertise materials they themselves manufactured. The Goodyear Rubber Company in the United States created a rubber doll in the 1920s specifically to bring its product to the public attention. In 1839, it was Charles Goodyear who had developed a process, which he termed vulcanization, by which rubber was made less brittle. Rubber, at least initially, was regarded as a perfect material to use in doll manufacture – it was virtually unbreakable – but it was soon discovered to be less than durable. One of the major problems was that of the paint flaking off; another was that rubber itself does deteriorate over time. Later, because of the durability problem, rubber was confined to the manufacture of dolls' bodies. As late as 1940, for example, a design known as the "Magic Skin Baby" was being made with a composition head fixed to a body of rubber filled with cotton and foam.

Nelson Goodyear, the inventor's brother, successfully gained a petition for a patent for a rubber dolls' head at the beginning of the 1850s; the heads were usually attached to cloth bodies. Licenses to produce dolls using Goodyear's product were granted to several companies, including the New York Rubber Co. and Benjamin F. Lee, which then marketed their dolls through stores.

Rubber was but one material whose popularity waxed and waned during this period. Celluloid in many ways had a similar history to rubber. At first, it seemed a perfect medium for doll manufacturers: it was lightweight, apparently robust, and could be molded and drilled. Unfortunately, it was discovered to have many drawbacks, not least that it was easily (and irreparably) deformed and also inflammable. Coloring faded over time too, espe-

dolls had composition heads mounted on cloth bodies, and the heads consisted of molded hair and painted features. Interestingly, the hands were very similar to those which had appeared on the earlier Campbell Kids designs. These dolls were heavily pushed by the salesmen: "with heads modeled from life by an American sculptress and such original models duly protected by copyright."

The craze for dolls that advertised a particular product or service was maintained by a series of dolls that were known as "Buddy Lees." Originally made from composition, they were subsequently made from more durable vinyl. The original dolls were made for the H. Q. Lee Jeans Company Inc. to advertise Lee jeans, and were a common sight from the 1920s to the end of the 1940s. The characters wore a variety of everyday work clothing, often with company logos for identification. They included such characters as a Gulf Oil worker, a Coca Cola delivery man, a cowboy, and a police officer.

Similar types of advertising dolls were also made in England during the interwar period. One of the better-known examples were the dolls produced to advertise Bisto, a type of dehydrated gravy compound, in the 1930s. The dolls (male and female versions were available) had the look of street urchins, and were dressed in ragged, plain-colored hand-me-down clothing. The dolls comprised composition heads and cloth bodies, and had a rather odd expression: their eyes were closed and they appeared to be savoring the aroma from a steaming bowl of reconstituted Bisto.

In general, advertising-based dolls did not travel well; they only appealed to the public of those countries in

Right: *A rubber character doll produced in England during the 1920s.*

Far right: *A Celluloid doll manufactured by France's Société Nobel Française, c.1920. Celluloid was first used in the 1870s and, although it did not flake, it was easily cracked and highly flammable.*

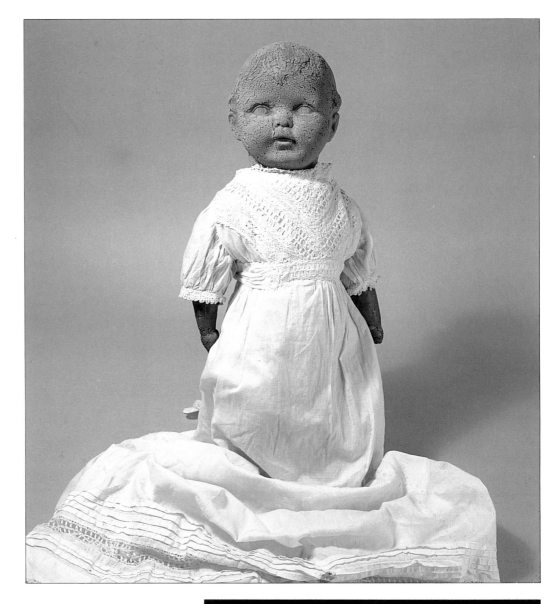

Below right: *A French celluloid doll from the 1920s.*

cially when subjected to prolonged exposure to direct sunlight. Although Celluloid was invented in the middle of the nineteenth century, its popularity was very much confined to the second half of that century. By the 1920s it was in terminal decline and had all but disappeared by the 1930s.

Celluloid was patented in the late 1860s by the Hyatt Brothers Company in the United States, which originally used Celluloid in the manufacture of billiard balls, though it is believed to have been invented in England. Its basis was a mixture of nitrocellulose and powdered camphor. In the doll-making process, sheets of Celluloid were molded and compressed by heat to produce often finely detailed heads. The centers for Celluloid dolls were in Germany, where companies such as Armand Marseille and Kestner took the lead, and France, where the Société Nobel Française (S.N.F.) and the Société Industrielle de Celluloid (S.I.C.) produced some fine dolls.

The S.I.C. merged with a number of other companies in the 1920s and was succeeded by the S.N.F. from 1927,

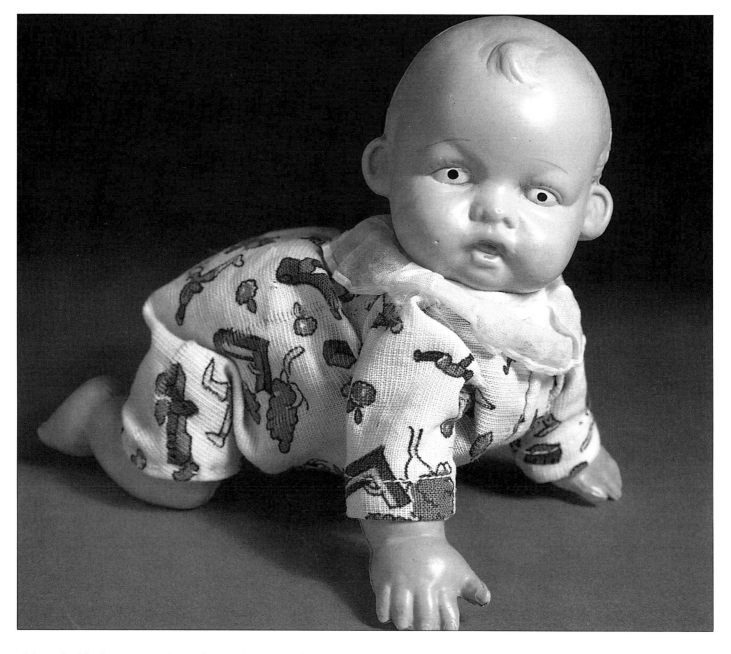

although this firm was only registered as a trading company on the eve of World War II. The latter company's dolls can be recognized by their logo of a mythical beast known as a wyvern, a marriage of a dragon and griffin.

In the United States, the first dolls in the medium are believed to have been made by the Celluloid Manufacturing Company in the early 1880s, though other companies such as Horsman also produced similar dolls from just before World War I. Celluloid dolls were also made in England but, like in the United States, in relatively small numbers. Japanese manufacturers created Celluloid dolls in very large quantities.

Dolls made in Celluloid were, as mentioned, produced in Germany. One of the leading companies was the Rheinische Gummi und Zelluloid Fabrik company based in Bavaria. Its wares can be recognized by the distinctive turtle trademark which is said to indicate the durability of

its dolls. The firm did not, however, just manufacture dolls under its own name, but often provided dolls for other manufacturers based on the molds created by the other companies. These Celluloid dolls can be identified by the fact that they carried the trading marks of both the Bavarian company and the provider of the mold.

Celluloid dolls do have certain similar characteristics. Heads are commonly of two types: either a swivel-type head fitted to a Celluloid or composition body, or a Celluloid head fitted to a rag body. In the latter case, the lower limbs are made from Celluloid. Typically, Celluloid dolls are recognizable by the distinctive glossy sheen that is produced by the material.

In England, one of the leading firms involved in the advertising and media-personality field was Dean's Rag Book Company Limited. The company, as its name suggests, produced illustrated books for children and a wide

Far left: *A Japanese-produced walking doll manufactured in Celluloid on the eve of World War II.*

Left: *An example of the type of doll produced by Dean's Rag Book Co., dating from c.1913. The firm's products were made was of printed cloth, and could be bought in kit form to be made up by the purchaser.*

range of rag dolls. By the 1920s, some two decades after it was founded, production techniques had improved, and the company felt confident enough to introduce a range of dolls under the umbrella name "True-to-Life."

Potential purchasers had two options: they could buy a ready-made version of a particular doll or, if more ambitious, could opt for a kit from which the dolls could be made at home. The variety of True-to-Life dolls was enormous, and they came both clothed and unclothed. One innovation of these dolls was that they had feet designed in such a way that they could stand unaided.

Dean's Rag Book Company, however, did not just manufacture this line of dolls. It was involved in every possible design: advertising dolls, Mickey Mouse and other cartoon-character dolls, notably a now somewhat rare Popeye the Sailor Man, and dolls in the flamboyant, highly decorative style of the Italian designer and manu-

facturer Lenci. One of the firm's most charismatic character dolls was that of a bookie's runner, which was offered to the public in the 1930s. Dressed in an appropriate tartan checked suit with scarlet vest, he had a moneybag slung over one shoulder, a prominent watch chain and whistle, and a pipe sticking out from the corner of his mouth. A hat set at a rakish angle completed the outfit, while an intriguing, slightly humorous, painted face gave the character an appropriate look for a horse-racing and betting man.

The other major English doll-making company – Chad Valley – also produced these character/advertising figures during the interwar period. One of the more common designs is that of a character who appeared in a cartoon strip associated with the English national newspaper the *Daily Mirror*, known as George. The cartoon was the creation of Tom Webster, and the felt doll was

Above: *Another example of a Dean's Rag Book doll – in this case, the ever-popular American cartoon character Popeye.*

Right: *A Dean's Rag Book Co. doll from the 1930s, exhibiting a more polished finish and more elegant clothing.*

Far right: *One of the most famous Chad Valley creations of the 1930s was "George." This figure was based on a cartoon-strip character that appeared in an English newspaper, the Daily Mirror.*

Right: *A superb character doll produced by Dean's Rag Book Co. in the 1930s, this bookie's runner is instantly recognizable as such.*

instantly recognizable by its extremely fluffy mustache, a derby hat set sloping across the head, and a cloth patch that advertised the paper and Webster's cartoon which was positioned over the doll's left breast. Other well-known Chad Valley cartoon characters from this era were those of the ever-mischievous Felix the cat and Bonzo the dog which, like George, appeared in a national newspaper, the *Daily Sketch*.

Chad Valley was also involved in the production of dolls that were said to be modeled on members of the British royal family. This was not a new tradition in doll-making in England: Queen Victoria was a popular subject for much of her reign, and some of the best examples from that era were produced by Madame Montanari, a woman of Italian extraction who had settled in London in the early years of the nineteenth century. The intense public excitement generated by the Great Exhibition of 1851, an exposition to reflect England and her empire's position, also prompted many Queen Victoria dolls.

In the 1930s, Chad Valley introduced dolls of Princess Elizabeth (later Elizabeth II) and her sister Margaret Rose (Princess Margaret). Interestingly, a German manufacturer, perhaps in recognition of the Windsor family's origins, also made a doll of Elizabeth as a toddler in 1929. The doll showed the future queen as a three-year-old, and was manufactured by Schoenau and Hoff-meister. The young princess was dressed in a frilly, smock-like outfit, and wore a straw boater. Royal characters, often introduced to coincide with a major event such as an anniversary or marriage, remain popular down to the present day.

The period between the end of World War I and the beginning of World War II saw many changes in the world of doll-making. Traditional centers of business, notably Germany and France, were, to a considerable extent, succeeded by the United States, a situation that remains true to the present. Secondly, previously well-established materials for the manufacture of dolls were,

Left: *A doll produced by Dean's in the 1930s. The company was also one of the earliest English manufacturers of teddy bears.*

to a greater or lesser extent, superseded by comparatively newer or more durable materials, particularly composition and cloth of various types. Not all the newer materials were successful, as was the case with Celluloid and rubber, though they were fashionable for a time.

The reasons for these changes are many, but a few general points can be made. Firstly, there was a shift in the use of dolls. Previously, they were often made as objects to be admired rather than played with. Many of the more traditional materials could simply not stand up to the rigors of children's play. Dolls were often very expensive items which only the fairly wealthy could afford. In the first 40 years or so of the twentieth century, as the relatively well-to-do middle classes grew in size, so too did the demand for dolls – but at a competitive price. Manufacturers responded to this call against a background of a general worldwide recession, and looked to use the cheaper materials.

Dolls before the twentieth century were often of what might be called "adult" designs, and were not necessarily likely to appeal to children. Character dolls began a move away from the older type of doll, and this was reinforced by other developments, notably the marketing of characters that would be familiar to children, such as those found in fairy tales or in the movies or other media. Other companies used dolls as a marketing tool to promote their particular wares, and these could be successful, at least for a short time.

By the time of World War II, therefore, the nature of doll-making had changed dramatically from that of the previous century. Many of the old designs and materials were still being used to produce very high-quality dolls, but new materials and characters were being introduced to capture a bigger share of a growing market. These trends would continue into the postwar world, and other changes would also provoke further major shifts in the look of doll manufacture, giving the public an even wider range of potential purchases to consider.

CHAPTER THREE

A New Generation

Left: *Mary Jane, one of the dolls produced by American company Effanbee in the late 1950s. She stands 36 inches tall.*

Above: *A hard-plastic walking doll with mohair hair produced by Palitoy in the late 1950s. She wears her original clothes.*

Left: *Pedigree's Princess doll from 1950. She has retained her original nylon clothes and has artificial hair comprising mohair.*

Right: *Another Pedigree creation. This time a walking African-American doll from the middle of the 1950s.*

Below: *A composition doll with sideways-glancing eyes and molded hair manufactured by Pedigree in the 1940s.*

Between 1925 and 1945, the great German companies that had dominated the world doll market for some 75 years lost their ascendancy, and new materials, new designers, and new manufacturers came to fore. The United States and Great Britain were leaders in the post-war development of dolls for a new generation of children and collectors-to-be.

The early promise of Celluloid, invented in England in the mid-nineteenth century, had not been fulfilled. This thin material, made of natural cellulose mixed with a solvent such as camphor, could be beautifully crafted, but it was easily squashed and, once crushed, could never be restored to its original shape. Rubber dolls, too, had limited durability, although many American manufacturers, beginning with Nelson Goodyear in the 1850s, had produced them. They also became popular in the U.K. Rubber seemed the ideal material for a plaything, in that it was soft and unbreakable and could be painted and molded. However, the colors on rubber doll heads faded over time, and the rubber decomposed, becoming shapeless, and making the features blurred and cracked. Eventually, only doll bodies were made of rubber, with heads made of less perishable materials.

The evolution of hard plastic during World War II brought major innovations to doll-making in the postwar years. By 1948 the Ideal Toy Company was producing the Baby Coos doll, with a hard-plastic head and composition limbs, for the American market. In 1951 Brother Coos was added to the line, soon followed by the Magic Skin Baby, stuffed with foam rubber and cotton. The hard-plastic dolls of good quality wore well, but low-grade plastic resulted in cracks along the seams, which also presented a safety hazard.

In the U.K., Pedigree Soft Toys Ltd. was the first company to use mass-production methods for high-quality composition dolls. By 1948 the firm was making Beauty Skin dolls with rubber bodies and hard-plastic heads. Eight years later, it introduced an all-plastic walking doll. The Rosebud Doll Company, founded in 1947 by Eric Smith, moved from composition to plastic dolls, and Smith invented a talking device that was very successful. His firm was finally acquired by the U.S.-based Mattel Corporation in 1967.

Above: *The English doll manufacturer Pedigree was renowned for its high-quality dolls. This example of its craft is plastic, has molded hair, and dates from the 1950s.*

Left: *A Pedigree boy doll with molded hair from the 1950s.*

Right: *A Rosebud Doll Company, England, plastic character doll, with "saron" hair, dating from 1955.*

Right: *A Linda Williams doll, probably from the 1950s, is based on a character from the television series, "Make Room for Daddy."*

Far right: *Dating from the 1950s, this Rosebud Doll Company doll has hair made from mohair and is wearing her original clothes.*

The British National Doll Company was making dolls with china heads before the war; afterward, it moved into hard-plastic dolls, including baby dolls with molded hair, open/shut eyes, and bent limbs jointed at hips, shoulders, and wrists. A typical 10-inch (25.4-cm) B.N.D. doll of the early 1950s came dressed in rompers with a pleated front. Pedigree also made an all-plastic baby doll with molded hair, a swivel head, and slightly bent arms and legs that moved from the shoulders and hips. The same head was used for the rubber Beauty Skin doll. Many of the all-plastic dolls were well cast but not as well finished, as the molding ridges were visible along the limbs and head.

New York's Alexander Doll Company had been in business successfully for 20 years when it adopted hard plastic in the 1940s. As always, Madame Alexander dolls in the new medium were both beautiful and well made, setting a standard for other American companies. With few exceptions, these dolls were marked on the head "Alexander/(year date)/number." The 18-inch (46-cm) Wendy

Ann doll of 1947 was unusual in having a human-hair wig of soft brown curls, which was surmounted by a large blue bow. She wore a pink-and-blue ruffled dress with a sprig of flowers at the waist, white anklets, and patent-leather Mary Jane shoes with bows. Wendy Ann had delicately colored features, open/shut eyes, a closed Cupid's-bow mouth, and a wistful expression that captivated doll lovers. Like all Madame Alexander's creations, she was acquired so eagerly that the stores could barely keep her in stock. The familiar pink-and-blue Alexander Doll Company boxes disappeared from the stores by word of mouth, although the company did advertise in selected media. The same mold used for the hard-plastic Wendy Ann doll was used for the Margaret O'Brien doll of 1947, modeled on the popular child movie star of the day. Other Madame Alexander hard-plastic character dolls of the late 1940s included the enchanting 14-inch (36-cm) Prince Charming, and Cinderella, ornaments to any collection. The prince wore a white satin doublet and cape trimmed in gold, a feathered satin cap, and

Left: *Originally purchased in one of Marks and Spencer's department stores in the late 1940s, this is a plastic doll manufactured by B.N.D. of London.*

Right: *Another B.N.D. doll from the 1950s made in plastic.*

Below: *A Roddy walking boy doll of the early 1950s with molded hair and painted eyes.*

taupe-colored tights with gold-buttoned shoes. Cinderella was gowned in white satin with a square-cut neckline and short puffed sleeves with ruffles. A crystal crown and hair net adorned her blonde hair.

During the early 1950s, Madame Alexander made a pair of dolls representing Queen Elizabeth II and Prince Philip, in honor of the queen's coronation. Later in the decade, a portrait doll of the queen in her coronation gown was produced in the popular line of Cissy dolls. These 21-inch-high fashion dolls for the older child came with a wide variety of meticulously designed wardrobes, from full-length evening gowns to delicate organza floral prints in pastel shades, with pumps, gloves, earrings, and hats to co-ordinate. A Cissy doll trademark was the tiny hatbox attached to the wrist by gold cord and inscribed "Madame Alexander, New York." Yardley of London used the stylish Cissy dolls to advertise its line of toiletries. A younger companion doll called Cissette became a popular addition to the Alexander doll family.

During the 1950s, the Alexander Doll Company diversified into plastic-and-vinyl and all-vinyl dolls. Mohair wigs, made from Angora goat hair, had been superseded

Right: *A Roddy teenage doll from 1958 comprising vinyl and hard plastic with "saron" hair.*

Far right: *An African-American Roddy doll in its original clothes from the early 1950s.*

by synthetic materials like saran, in which the hairstyle was permanently set by heat, and by Dynel and nylon, which could be water-set by the child. Synthetic hair was sewn by machine to a net base and glued to the heads of hard-plastic dolls. The development of soft vinyl enabled manufacturers to produce dolls with rooted nylon wigs that could be washed, cut, and styled. The vinyl bodies were soft, unbreakable, and washable, and could be finely cast for realistic detail.

The Madeline doll, from Madame Alexander in 1952, came with comb and curlers for styling her shoulder-length hair. Ball-jointed at wrist, shoulder, hip, and knee, Madeline wore a ruffled white organza dress with a lavender velvet sash and a straw hat trimmed with lavender ribbons and flowers. That same year, Madame Alexander won the coveted Fashion Academy award for her dolls for the second time in a row. Other Alexander dolls of the early 1950s included Rosebud, a soft-plastic baby doll with voice and moving eyes; the Diaper Baby Doll, which drank from a bottle and could be changed; the delightful Annabelle doll, modeled on a character from the popular pioneering television show hosted by singer Kate Smith; and the Maggie Walker walking doll, which a child could lead by the hand. Annabelle had open/shut eyes, a closed mouth, painted lower lashes, rooted synthetic hair with ribbons on either side of the head, and a monogrammed skirt-and-sweater set. The doll was available in several different sizes.

Madame Alexander produced several Disney character dolls during the 1950s, including a 14-inch (35.6-cm) hard-plastic Peter Pan and, in 1959, a blue-and-silver-gowned Sleeping Beauty, sold at the Disneyland complex in California and Spiegel's department store. There was also a now-rare Peter Pan Quiz-Kin, with two buttons on the back that made the head shake "yes" and "no." Like the Disney Peter Pan, the Quiz-Kins wore short pointed tunics over tights and pointed, feathered caps. The 10-inch (25.4-cm) Sleeping Beauty doll was from the Cissette mold.

In 1953 the popular Alexander-kins line of baby dolls was introduced, including a blonde baby with open/closed mouth, large open/shut eyes with painted lower lashes, and a ruffled cap that matched her polka-dot pinafore. The eight-inch (20-cm) dolls were produced for many years in a variety of styles and costumes.

Another Alexander doll based on a popular television character was the 14-inch (35.6-cm) Shari Lewis doll of 1959. All plastic except for vinyl arms, she was completely jointed, with painted features and pierced ears for pearl-drop earrings. Her long auburn hair was drawn back into a cascade of curls with a small ponytail at the crown and curly bangs, and she had hazel/green sleeping eyes with molded lashes. Contemporary with her was the eight-inch (20-cm) Little Genius doll, with a vinyl

body and a hard-plastic head. An open mouth/nurser baby doll, she had a caracul blonde wig and sleeping eyes.

Vinyl had been used more widely by all the major companies during the 1950s, as seen in the 22-inch (53-cm) Kelly doll of the late 1950s, which carried a small matching Wendy doll in hard plastic. The Wendy doll was a straight-leg walker that came in various sizes, similar in design to the bent-knee walking Lissy doll introduced by Alexander in 1954.

The Ideal Toy Corporation, founded by Morris Mitchtom in 1902, had prospered with its line of stuffed toys, and children of the postwar baby-boom generation found much to love in its imaginative and well-made playthings. During the 1950s and 1960s, Ideal produced a host of licensed and character dolls in collaboration with major U.S. companies like Revlon, Gillette (Toni home permanents), *McCall*'s magazine, and others. The same molds were sometimes used for lower-priced non-licensed products.

During the 1950s, Ideal reprised its 1930s Shirley Temple doll, representing America's favorite child star

Left: *Lissy, a bent-knee walking doll dating from 1956 and produced by Madame Alexander.*

Right: *Prince Charles by Madame Alexander, a bent-leg walking doll measuring eight inches, from the latter part of the 1950s.*

Left: *Two famous dolls produced by Madame Alexander in the middle of the 1950s: the 20-inch-tall Cissy (left), and Cissette (10.5 inches). Note the matching costumes.*

Right: *Wendy, by Madame Alexander dates from the 1950s, is a straight-leg walking doll, and measures eight inches.*

of the Depression years. She became equally popular with postwar children through the new medium of television, and Ideal produced several different-sized Shirley Temple dolls in vinyl, with rooted hair in blonde curls, open/shut hazel eyes, and an open mouth with four teeth. The 19-inch (48-cm) version came dressed in a plaid jumper with a pearl-buttoned green bolero jacket and a red hair ribbon. She was an unmistakable likeness of the winsome child star at the age of six or seven years.

Perhaps the best-known American doll of the 1950s was Ideal's Toni doll, produced by arrangement with the Gillette Company. This hard-plastic doll with "magic Nylon hair" came with her own Play-Wave kit for washing and setting her hair. The 20-inch (51-cm) model wore a plaid jumper trimmed with rickrack, and a nylon blouse with full-length puffed sleeves, trimmed with ruffles and red buttons. She wore white anklets and red Mary Jane shoes and had movable arms, open/shut eyes, and a closed mouth. A 14-inch (36-cm) Toni doll had brunette hair topped by a flat red bow, and wore a red pina-

fore with floral embroidery and a yellow blouse with short puffed sleeves trimmed in lace and rickrack. Tiny red Mary Jane shoes and yellow-and-white anklets completed the attractive ensemble. This hard-plastic doll was tagged at the wrist "Be Proud of Your Toni Doll," and was widely advertised in department-store catalogs. (From the same attractive mold Ideal produced the Sara Ann doll, with rooted saran hair instead of nylon. Sara Ann wore a floral-print waffle-piqué dress with short puffed sleeves and a sheer white pinafore edged in green rickrack with a flat green hairbow to match.) The Toni dolls were an instant success and added greatly to the effect of the Gillette Company's adult advertising campaign for its home-permanent line, "Which Twin has the Toni?"

Another non-licensed doll that used the Toni face was Ideal's enchanting Princess Mary doll of the early 1950s. She had a vinyl head with rooted hair in brown bangs, trimmed with pastel flowers on each side and mauve ribbons. Her elegant cream-colored dress had puffed net

Left: *A Shari Lewis doll by Madame Alexander consisting of hard-plastic and vinyl arms. The doll, dating from 1959, is completely jointed, including at the waist. She has painted features, and pierced ears with pearl-drop earrings. Shari Lewis was a notable television star of the period.*

Below: *Sleeping Beauty, one of the best-loved fairy-tale characters, as produced by Madame Alexander, comprising hard plastic with jointed knees. She measures 10 inches.*

sleeves edged in pink, and a net overskirt with a pink-ribbon waistline trimmed with tiny artificial flowers to match those in her hair. Her body was of hard plastic with movable arms and legs.

The Toni face also graced the Miss Curity doll – a nurse doll with a first-aid kit full of Curity products, and a package of curlers for setting her rooted nylon hair. Advertised as "the First Lady of First Aid," Miss Curity wore a white waffle-piqué nurse's cap with her name on it over shoulder-length blonde hair. Her matching white uniform had long cuffed sleeves and buttoned diagonally down the front, from neckline to flared hem. She had a short navy-blue cape that tied at the neck.

Another popular Ideal licensed doll was the Bakelite hard-plastic Betsy McCall, which had a vinyl head stuffed with cotton batting and a glued-on wig of short brunette hair, open/shut brown eyes, and a closed smiling mouth. The Betsy McCall character was used by *McCall's* magazine for its clothing patterns, and the doll came with its own printed pattern for making an apron. She was

Left: *A pair of Betsy McCall dolls in their original, late 1950s, costumes.*

Below: *A pair of Miss Toni dolls from the late 1950s.*

Above: *A 14-inch Linda Williams doll based on a character in the television series "Make Room for Daddy."*

Right: *A Betsy McCall doll of the 1950s in its original clothing.*

Far right: *Little Genius, by Madame Alexander, has a vinyl body with a hard-plastic head and blue-gray eyes with molded lashes. Its features are painted and it is eight inches tall.*

dressed in a red pinafore with white buttons, and a white blouse with short puffed sleeves and a Peter Pan collar. White anklets and black Mary Jane shoes completed her costume.

Ideal's Mary Hartline doll was modeled on a television star of the early 1950s known as the "Pretty Princess" of television. This hard-plastic doll, from the Toni mold, bore a striking resemblance to the attractive blonde Mary Hartline herself. The doll was dressed in a long-sleeved red dress with a flared skirt, imprinted in white with a musical staff. A white heart with the name "Mary" was imprinted on the bodice. She wore white majorette boots with gold tassels, trimmed in red, and had long blonde hair crowned by a red ribbon.

One of the first teenage fashion dolls was Ideal's Revlon, produced in association with the famous cosmetics company of the same name. Made entirely of vinyl, the Revlon doll was advertised as a "A Teen Age Sister with a Real Girl's Figure," and came with high-heeled shoes, sheer nylon stockings, high-fashion clothes, and elegant jewelry. Revlon could be bent and posed, and had red-painted fingernails and toenails and long curly hair. She had open/shut eyes with molded lashes, delicate eyebrows, and a closed mouth, and came in several different sizes.

The 22-inch (56-cm) Revlon doll could be purchased with a pink taffeta party dress with a dropped waist and short, puffed sleeves edged in ruffles. She wore a pearly necklace and her fingers were flared to display her elegant gathered skirt. Other models came in floral-print dresses of net and nylon, some with flower-trimmed straw hats and pearl-drop earrings to match their necklaces. The Revlon doll was soon joined by the 10-inch (25-cm) Little Miss Revlon, a forerunner of Mattel's famous Barbie doll, which could be purchased with several different boxed outfits.

Since Ideal had started out as a plush-toy company specializing in teddy bears, it was appropriate that it should also produce Smokey, "the Forest Fire Prevention Bear," in the early 1950s. Designed for both girls and boys, the stuffed Smokey doll came with a smiling plastic face and a fire-fighter's hat and shovel.

The American Character Doll Company, founded in 1918, made some of the best-known dolls of the 1950s and 1960s, including an all-vinyl Toni doll, after it took over the license from Ideal. American Character Doll's Toni doll was an older, more sophisticated-looking doll, growing up along with her owner. She had large open/shut blue eyes with molded lashes, and a closed mouth with a full underlip. A 14-inch (36-cm) 1959 model came dressed in a black-and-white striped dress topped by a red tunic, belted and bowed in black. She wore high-heeled black sandals with rhinestone trim, and a red-and-black hat over rooted shoulder-length hair that curled up on each side of her face. She carried a matching hatbox attached to her wrist by a patent-leather strap. The Toni doll also came in a 10-inch (25-cm) size to compete with Ideal's Little Miss Revlon. One popular version wore a blue taffeta dress with short sleeves and a bateau neck, trimmed near the puffed hem with a blue velvet bow. She wore a fur hat over blonde curls and carried a small fur muff.

The mold used for the Toni dolls was the same as that used for American Character Doll's Sweet Sue line of hard-plastic dolls, which had come out in the early 1950s. An early toddler Sweet Sue had open/shut blue eyes, a closed mouth, and light-brown curly hair trimmed with red flowers under a straw hat. She wore a red satin short-sleeved dress with lace-and-piqué collar and cuffs, white buttons, and a black velvet bow at the neck. A Sweet Sue walking doll of the same period was available as Alice in Wonderland, in a blue dress with white pinafore, white anklets, and patent-leather Mary Jane shoes. She had a curly blonde saran wig with bangs, and a blue ribbon that matched the one on her pinafore.

Another hard-plastic Sweet Sue doll came with a saran chignon hairpiece designed by the famous hairdresser Charles of the Ritz. She was advertised by the Saran Yarns Company as having "soft Saran hair that curls and waves without any special lotion or kit. You can give her all the newest hairdos: Pompadour, topknot, whirltop, halo, and many more." This attractive doll wore a full-length flounced plaid dress trimmed with ribbons, and had a small hatbox attached to her wrist for the chignon hairpiece. A 20-inch (51-cm) version of this doll was dressed in a short blue piqué frock trimmed in white lace and pink-and-blue artificial flowers. She had short curly brown hair and wore a wide-brimmed straw hat and taupe-colored ankle-strap shoes with blue buttons. There was also an 18-inch (46-cm) Sweet Sue walker, dressed in a floor-length ball gown of net and taffeta trimmed with ribbons.

Late in the 1950s, during its decade in business, the American Character Doll Co. took over the Betsy McCall license and produced a delightful line of Betsy McCall dolls in all vinyl. The schoolgirl model wore a white felt jumper trimmed in rickrack over a yellow-and-white short-sleeved dress, with red tights and ankle-strap patent-leather shoes. She had a white felt cap to match the jumper, which had a black bow to which a small red slate with white sums written on it was attached. A very successful addition to the line was an eight-inch (20-cm) all-hard-plastic subteen Betsy McCall, which was advertised as "America's Newest Glamour Girl." More than 100 different outfits could be purchased for her. There were also Betsy McCall gift sets, including the Designer's Studio, which included several outfits and accessories on different themes.

Sweet Sue also grew up over the years, evolving into an all-vinyl Sweet Sue Sophisticate, with limbs that could be posed, and rooted hair. She was tagged at the wrist with a pink-and-black poodle cutout.

The Vogue Doll Company was founded by Jennie Graves in 1922, and became known for the well-made clothing it produced for antique dolls imported from Germany. In the postwar years, Mrs. Graves introduced her famous Ginny dolls – a toddler doll with painted blue eyes

Far left: *A Madame Alexander doll, Caroline, dated 1961. It is all vinyl with rooted blonde hair. Several costume sets were available for this doll, including this two-piece pink party dress.*

Left: *An Alice Lon doll from the Lawrence Welk T.V. show in the late 1950s. The doll is 21 inches tall and completely jointed, even at the ankles, so that it can assume dancing poses.*

and closed mouth, made of hard plastic and named for the doll-maker's daughter, Virginia Graves Carlson. Sleeping eyes were introduced in 1951, and a walking model, with a beguiling stuffed terrier from Steiff, came out in 1954. The Ginny dolls were produced in a number of different materials and costumes, including a Tyrolean version.

Advertised as "Fashion Leaders in Doll Society," the Vogue dolls lived up to their promise in a long series of named and storybook dolls. A brother-and-sister set, Eve and Steve, wore matching plaid outfits with red sweaters and red-trimmed plaid hats. Made of hard plastic, they had sleeping eyes, closed mouths, delicate coloring, and blond wigs. Other named models included Linda, Wanda, and Ginny's baby sister, Ginnette, which

had an inflatable plastic pool set. During the late 1950s, Ginny's older sister, Jill, along with teenaged Jeff, were introduced. Jill wore a black-and-white dress imprinted with "Jill's Record Hop," and had strawberry-blonde curly hair, earrings, and high-heeled sandals. Jeff had molded brown hair and wore a plaid shirt and tan pants with brown shoes.

Another Ginny playset of the time featured kitchen appliances, with Ginny dressed in a cowgirl's outfit and Jill in a pink polka-dot sundress trimmed with lace and ribbons. Later, Jill was produced in vinyl in a variety of period costumes, including that of a pilgrim.

The Ginny doll was widely copied by other manufacturers, including Virga, during the 1950s. Virga advertised it as the Virga Playmates Walking Doll.

Far left: *A trio of Nancy Ann Storybook dolls, measuring five inches in height and dressed in assorted colorful dresses.*

Above: *A Nancy Ann Storybook doll measuring a mere two inches, made from hard plastic and dressed in a christening costume.*

Left: *A Sweet Sue doll made by the American Character Doll Company in the mid-1950s. The doll is made of hard plastic and measures 18 inches.*

Fleischaker & Baum (whose trademark was Effanbee) had been producing high-quality American dolls since 1910. By the postwar era, it was in vigorous competition with the Alexander Doll Company for the higher-priced end of the market. Effanbee's all-hard-plastic Honey doll, with nylon hair, open/shut eyes, and open/closed mouth was extremely attractive, as was the company's line of Little Lady dolls. One version of the Honey doll came with clothing designed by the French couture house of Schiaparelli. Effanbee's storybook and character dolls included an all-hard-plastic Prince Charming and Cinderella set, comparable in quality to that marketed by Madame Alexander.

Effanbee's Prince Charming wore a pink satin doublet trimmed with gold, and a short white cape lined with pink satin. He had a feathered white satin cap, and white hose with patent-leather pumps trimmed with rhinestone buckles. His blond wig was a shorter version of Cinderella's shoulder-length curls. Cinderella was dressed in a pink satin ball gown trimmed with ruffles and gold braid with pink net panniers set off by an artificial rose. She wore a gold crown and was tagged "Cinderella: An EFFANBEE Adorable Doll."

The E. I. Horsman Doll Company, founded in New York City in about 1865, had been acquired by the Royal Doll Company of Trenton, New Jersey, in 1940. Well known for its character and celebrity dolls, Horsman had sought technical alternatives to the cumbersome composition doll, and came up with a series of new materials that were widely used in the doll industry from the postwar years on. The first development was called "vinyl-plastic" – lightweight, unbreakable, and easily molded for realistic detail. Horsman research of the 1950s resulted in an even more pliable substance that the company called Super-Flex: it enabled the doll to be positioned in many different ways, including kneeling. Other developments were the lifelike Fairy Skin and Softee Skin vinyls, which were used to excellent effect by Horsman's sole designer of the period, Irene Szor. The company that had pioneered "Can't Break 'Em" composition dolls in the early 1900s thus retained its leadership position in the technology of doll-making.

Most Horsman dolls of the period 1940-present are marked, and sometimes dated, on the base of the head. Marks include "Horsman Doll Mfg. Co.," "Horsman-Dolls, Inc.," "A/Horsman/Doll," and "Irene Szor/Horsman." The popular Bright Star doll was originally a composition doll which evolved into hard plastic with glassine sleep eyes in the early 1950s. Literally dozens of models were available, some with open mouths showing teeth, others with closed mouths, and most (from 1952) with saran wigs in various colors and lengths. The line included the named dolls Alice, Gretchen, and Pigtail Peggy, in a variety of costumes including Party, Bride,

Bridesmaid, Skater, and Majorette. Some of these dolls were also available as African-American dolls.

Accessories were an important selling point with Horsman, which used them extensively in the 1950s. Dolls of this era came with both miniature and lifesize advertising products, including bars of Ivory Soap, Even-flo nursing bottles, miniature Carnation Milk cans, and others. The company's best-known dolls include those modeled on the Campbell's Kids soup commercials. A 1950 version of the famous pair, designed for boys and girls, was made of composition, with painted eyes and closed slit mouth (no lips). Fully jointed, with swivel heads, the dolls had painted hair and painted shoes and stockings. Some Campbell's Kids dolls were dressed in the traditional rompers, with white apron and a white chef's hat imprinted with a *C*. Others wore regular toddler-doll costumes, with a cap for the boy and a hair-bow for the girl. In 1953 they became available in the new soft-vinyl Fairy Skin material, with painted eyes and molded hair. That same year, Horsman introduced its Shadow Wave doll from the Bright Star mold, which came with hair-setting lotion, brush, comb, sponge, barrette, and curlers. This doll had a hard-plastic body and a

Far left: *Jeff, manufactured by the American Vogue Doll Company in the 1950s, is 12 inches tall.*

Left: *Poor Pitiful Pearl, a doll made by BrookGlad in 1957.*

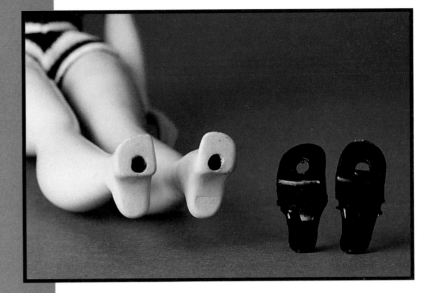

Left: *Undoubtedly the most
popular and successful doll
of all time, Barbie,
manufactured by Mattel,
was introduced in 1959 and
revolutionized the doll
world. These are the first in
the series.*

Above: *The original Barbie
had holes in her feet for a
stand, while the second had
a stand which could be
positioned under her arms.*

soft-vinyl Fairy Skin head with glassine eyes and a closed
mouth. It had a Dynel wig in blonde or brunette, a swivel
head, and fully jointed limbs. The Shadow Wave doll
came in four sizes, beginning at 14 inches (35.6 cm).

Baby dolls retained their hold on little girls' hearts
throughout the postwar era, and Horsman offered a wide
variety of these dolls, with voice boxes, "heartbeats,"
movable limbs, and other features. These included the
lifelike Tynie Baby of 1951, with soft-vinyl plastic head
and arms, cloth body, and legs stuffed with cotton. The
mouth was open, with teeth and tongue showing, and the
two largest models had a crying voice box. Another
popular baby doll of the day was the Tiny Tears doll, with
crying and wetting features, developed in the U.K. by
Palitoy, and marketed in the United States by the
American Character Doll Company. In the U.S., Tiny
Tears was available with a hard-plastic head and vinyl
body, and in all vinyl in various sizes from 1955 to 1962.
The doll came in a wardrobe trunk with several changes
of clothing and accessories, including a package of Kleenex tissues.

All-cloth Raggedy Ann and Andy dolls, designed by
Johnny B. Gruelle in 1915, have been popular ever since,
and many companies have manufactured them, including
Applause Dolls, Hasbro (Playskool label), Ideal, and
Mollye Dolls. Most familiar to the baby-boom gener-
ation, perhaps, are the Knickerbocker Raggedy Ann and
Andy dolls with red yarn hair, painted features including

black eyes outlined in white with lashes well below the eyes, triangular red noses, and smiling mouths. Both dolls have red-and-white striped legs and black feet.

Celebrity dolls were popular throughout the 1950s. A character on the Arthur Godfrey television variety show inspired the attractive hard-plastic Lu Ann Simms walking doll from the Roberta Doll Company. She had open/shut eyes, a long brunette wig, an open mouth with teeth, and a swivel neck. Jointed at hips and shoulders, she wore a blue piqué dress trimmed with pink rickrack, and a black velvet, flower-trimmed ribbon around her neck. She carried a black monogrammed shoulder bag. Other attractive hard-plastic dolls of this type were manufactured by the Arranbee Doll Company, creator of Nanette; the Royal Doll Company; the Terri Lee Sales Corporation, whose dolls were modeled on Terri Lee and her daughters, Connie Lynn and Linda, and whose line included the Jerri Lee boy doll; and Nancy Ann Storybook and Style Show Dolls. The Storybook dolls came in both painted bisque and hard plastic, while the Style Show dolls were all of hard plastic and dressed in ball gowns. Nancy Ann also offered a 10-inch (25.4-cm) baby doll made entirely of vinyl. An open mouth/nurser doll with blue sleep eyes, it was marked on the head NANCY ANN.

Other manufacturers of the early baby-boom years produced well-made dolls that are hard to find today. Some were sold in supermarkets, like the Candy Fashion Doll (in the Revlon doll mode), produced by the Deluxe Reading Company. The doll's box converted into a wardrobe for additional outfits and accessories. The Candy Fashion doll of 1957 was all vinyl, with jointed elbows and knees. She had blue sleep eyes, human hair, and pierced ears. Deluxe Toys (no longer in business) was the parent company for five other firms, including Deluxe Topper, Topper Corp., Topper Toys, and Deluxe Toy Creations. Most of their dolls were marked on the head with one of these names.

One of the most successful American toy companies was founded in 1945 by Elliot and Ruth Handler and Harold Matson: the name "Mattel" was formed by combining syllables from their names. Originally, dollhouses were Mattel's major product, but it soon diversified and prospered as a result of its pioneering advertising campaign on ABC-TV's "Mickey Mouse Club." It was Ruth Handler who conceived the idea of a teenage fashion doll from Mattel. The result was Barbie, whose runaway success began in 1959 with a $1 Barbie – now a prized collector's item. She was all vinyl, with rooted hair, painted eyes, pierced ears, closed mouth, and high-heeled feet with holes in them. Jointed at neck, shoulders, and hips, she was 11½ inches (29 cm) tall, and had a blonde or

Right: *Lullaby Baby was produced by Horsman in the late 1950s.*

Far right: *Raggedy Ann is one of the longest-lived dolls, and one of the most successful. This example dates from the 1950s.*

brunette ponytail and bangs, blue eyeliner, arched eyebrows, and colorless irises. Until 1952 she was marked on the right hip: "Barbie/Pats. Pend./©MCMLVIII/by Mattel Inc."

The original Barbie doll wore the now-famous black-and-white-knit maillot bathing suit and came with white sunglasses with blue lenses, black open-toed shoes, and hoop earrings. She was packaged with a pronged stand, and the shoes created for her first ensembles had holes at the ball of the foot for the insertion of the prongs into the holes in her feet.

Twenty-one different outfits with accessories were available for Barbie in 1959, some of which were carried into the early 1960s. One of the best-known is the Roman Holiday travel ensemble. It included a belted dress with a red-and-white striped top, and a matching ribbed coat.

Other accessories were a tiny brass compact engraved with a *B*, a white plastic purse, black-rimmed glasses in a white-and-clear plastic case, a "pearl" on a chain necklace, short white tricot gloves, a plastic comb, and a handkerchief. Other notable wardrobe items from Barbie's debut included the Gay Parisienne bubble dress in blue pindot rayon taffeta; the Plantation Belle waltz-length party dress in pink sheer dotted fabric with lace-and-braid ruffles; and the Easter Parade ensemble, with an apple-print sheath dress, black faille coat, and a headband hat fashioned from a silk organza bow. The meticulous detail of both clothes and accessories set a high standard that Mattel would live up to in the years to come.

CHAPTER FOUR

Barbie and Friends

Left: *Mattel's Fashion Queen Barbie, complete with original packaging, from 1963.*

Above: *Ideal Toy's Corporation's response to the success of Barbie was Tammy (left), released in 1962. A year later, a "family" was introduced, including brother Ted (right).*

Above: *A pair of Mattel's Charmin' Chatty dolls with a young admirer. They were the prototype for the popular Chatty Cathy line of pull-string talking dolls.*

Mattel took a leadership position among U.S. doll-makers with the unprecedented success of Barbie and a host of other imaginative and innovative dolls of the 1960s, including the Chatty Cathy series of talking dolls, Baby First Step, and the diminutive Kiddles line.

The #2 Barbie came out in 1959 and was identical to #1 except that there were no holes in the bottom of her feet. Two models were added to the line in 1960-61: #3 Barbie, which had blue irises and curved eyebrows (some with brown instead of blue eyeliner), and #4, in which the skin tone of the original models no longer faded to a pale color. Over the next few years, new hair colors and styles were added, bendable knees were introduced, and in 1967 Barbie got a new face. Meanwhile, the 12-inch (31-cm) Ken doll had been added in 1961, first with flocked hair, then with painted hair. Barbie's best friend, Midge, came out in 1962 (using the Barbie's body and mark), closely followed by the 9-inch (23-cm) Skipper and Skooter dolls – Barbie's little sister and her friend.

Six new outfits were added to Barbie's wardrobe in 1960, along with 19 continued from the previous year. The Busy Gal ensemble equipped Barbie as a fashion de-

Above right: *Charmin' Chatty pictured in natural surroundings and dressed in the popular sailor-suit outfit.*

signer, with a red linen suit, black-rimmed glasses, and a monogrammed portfolio of her designs. In 1961 Barbie became a stewardess for American Airlines, with a smart blue suit and hat and a zippered flight bag with the airline's insignia. Throughout the decade, new outfits and accessories, interchangeable for Barbie and Midge, were added to the line. In 1965 Skipper's new friend Ricky joined the Barbie family, with four new outfits of his own. The following year brought Tutti and Todd – twin toddlers – and Barbie's mod cousin Francie, who wore the newest fashions from London's Carnaby Street. In 1967 Francie became available as an African-American doll. The high quality of Mattel's designs never faltered as new dolls and costumes were added to the line, and Barbie was equally successful abroad, with some costumes available only in foreign countries.

During the early 1960s, Mattel introduced Charmin' Chatty, a prototype of the popular all-vinyl Chatty Cathy line of pull-string talking dolls. These endearing 20-inch (50.9-cm)-tall freckle-faced dolls were remarkably lifelike, with a wide-eyed expression, snub nose, and open/closed smiling mouth with teeth. Chatty Cathy was available as a blonde or brunette, with hairstyles including side ponytails and bangs. A limited number of African-American Chatty Cathy dolls were produced wearing children's clothing – short bibbed dresses or pinafores, with anklets and sandals or flat shoes.

In 1962 Tiny Chatty Baby Sister and Brother appeared in the 15-inch (38.1-cm) size, with colorful rompers, caps, bootees, and monogrammed bibs. Like Chatty Cathy, they had large, sleeping eyes with molded lashes and open/closed mouths with two teeth. There was also a Singing Chatty doll. In 1962, Shrinking Violet joined the Mattel line. She was a 15-inch (38.1-cm) cloth doll with yarn hair whose features moved when she "talked," activated by a pull string.

Mattel's 24-inch (61-cm) Dancerina doll had a plastic body and legs with vinyl arms and head. The African-American Dancerina doll had brown painted eyes and African-American rather than Caucasian features. These dolls wore a tutu, tights, and toeshoes, and their action was controlled by a knob on top of the head in the form of a tiara.

Throughout the decade, Mattel added to its baby and toddler doll lines with such dolls as Baby First Step, an

SKOOTER®

RICKY™

MIDGE®

KEN®

CASEY™

TV PRINT

MIDGE #0860
Close companion! Standard with bathing suit, three hair colors. 11½″ tall.
Std. Pack: 1 Doz.   Wt: 9 Lbs.

SKIPPER WITH LIFELIKE BENDABLE LEGS #1030
Cute playmate! Three hair colors. Swimsuit, hairband, comb and brush. 9¼″ tall.
Std. Pack: 1 Doz.   Wt: 7 Lbs.

SKIPPER #0950
Standard. Swimsuit, three hair colors. Headband, comb and brush. 9½″ tall.
Std. Pack: 1 Doz.   Wt: 6 Lbs.

SKOOTER, SKIPPER'S FRIEND #1040
Playful pigtail personality! Standard with swimsuit, three hair colors. 9¼″ tall.
Std. Pack: 1 Doz.   Wt: 6 Lbs.

NEW! CHRIS, TUTTI'S FRIEND #3570
Braided beauty! Rooted hair in two colors, poseable. 7⅝″ tall.
Std. Pack: 1 Doz.   Wt: 4 Lbs.

NEW! TUTTI, BARBIE & SKIPPER'S TINY SISTER #3580
New charm and new outfit! Blonde or brunette hair, poseable. 7⅝″ tall.
Std. Pack: 1 Doz.   Wt: 4 Lbs.

NEW! TODD #3590
In open stock! Popular and poseable little lad in sport outfit. Rooted hair, 7⅝″ tall.
Std. Pack: 1 Doz.   Wt: 4 Lbs.

KEN #0750
An All-American guy! Standard with trunks and beach jacket. Molded hair, 12½″ tall.
Std. Pack: 1 Doz.   Wt: 9 Lbs.

RICKY, SKIPPER'S FRIEND #1090
Cutest freckle-faced lad in town! 9¼″ tall in beach jacket, trunks.
Std. Pack: 1 Doz.   Wt: 6 Lbs.

#0860   #1030   #0950   #1040   #3570   #3580   #3590   #0750   #1090

"TUTTI & TODD, BARBIE & SKIPPER'S TINY TWIN SISTER & BROTHER" are the trademarks of Mattel, Inc. for its DOLLS.

Left: *An advertisement illustrating the growing range of Barbie's friends. Here, from left to right, are Casey, Skooter, Ricky, Midge, and boyfriend Ken.*

Right: *Mattel's Julia was introduced in 1969.*

Below: *"The World of Barbie," including, from left to right: Francie, Todd, Tutti, Chris, and Skipper.*

BARBIE®

FRANCIE™

TODD®

TUTTI®

CHRIS™

SKIPPER®

18-inch (46-cm) toddler which was also available as a talking doll; Cheerful Tearful, which changed expression; Baby Say 'N' See and Baby Secret (1965); Baby Small Talk; and Randy Reader, a battery-operated doll with eyes that moved from side to side as she read a book about the children's character Strawberry Shortcake. The popular Baby Tenderlove was introduced in 1969 as a 13-inch (33-cm) newborn, and as a 16-inch (40.6-cm) talking doll.

Another major Mattel success began in 1966, with the introduction of a line of tiny dolls with oversized heads packaged with a great variety of accessories – the Kiddles. Ranging in size from a half-inch (1.4-cm) Kiddle in a child's ring to three-and-a-half inches (nine cm), these engaging dolls were eagerly welcomed by children, who collected them for years. The Storybook Kiddles came with a storybook and jewelry in a heart-shaped box, and featured sweethearts like Romeo and Juliet, Robin Hood and Maid Marian and Rapunzel.

Above: *Shrinking Violet, another of Mattel's lines, was introduced in 1962. A cloth doll with yarn hair, her features moved when she talked, activated by a pull-string mechanism.*

Far left: *A pair of Mattel Chatty Cathy dolls. The doll was available as either a blonde or a brunette, styled with either side ponytails or bangs.*

Left: *Cynthia, a talking doll, was introduced by Mattel in the 1960s.*

There were character Kiddles like Santa Claus, animal Kiddles, and a host of named Kiddles like Baby Biddle, which came with a baby carriage, and Rolly Twiddle, which had a wagon, pail and shovel. Then there were Lois Locket, Lickety Spiddle, Sizzly Friddle, and many others, with accessories including toy cars, airplanes, ice-cream cones, cola bottles, cologne bottles, and full-sized teacups and saucers (for the Tea Party Kiddles, including the elegant little Lady Silver, Lady Lavender, and others named by color). The Skediddles were the largest dolls in the line.

In 1963 the American Character Doll Co. introduced its own teenage fashion doll in response to Barbie. This was Tressy, which had a key in her back that made her hair "grow," and came with her own hair-care magazine, *Hair Glamour*, and directions for creating six different hairstyles. The original 12½-inch (32-cm) Tressy wore heavy make-up, but Tressy #2 (1965-66) was introduced as Mary Magic Make-up, and came with a pale face and no lashes, to be made up by the child. Neither doll

was a commercial success. However, the American Character Doll Co. (which also used the name American Doll and Toy Company from 1959) carried the Sweet Sue doll into the early 1960s and added an all-vinyl Tiny Tears doll in 1963. The Toodles line, from baby to toddler to child, was joined in 1961 by the 18-inch (46-cm) Toodle-Loo doll, and the American Character Doll Co. entered the burgeoning talking-doll market with Talking Marie, a vinyl-and-plastic doll with a battery-operated record player inside. In 1965 Sally Says, a 19-inch (48.3-cm) plastic-and-vinyl doll, became available.

The Alexander Doll Company continued to create beautiful dolls and new lines throughout the 1960s. Madame Alexander created dolls based on characters from favorite children's stories, famous people, and heroines from popular adult fiction like Scarlett O'Hara of *Gone With the Wind*, along with the child and baby characters original to the company. Its initial success had been built on muslin Alice in Wonderland dolls and the composition Dionne Quintuplet dolls of the late 1930s, in-

Far left: *A set of miniature dolls from Mattel's Kiddles series. This is part of the comparatively rare Peter Pandiddle set – Tinkerbell and Crocodile – from 1967.*

Left: *Howard "Biff" Boodle from the Kiddles range is a rare doll, produced for one year only – 1966.*

Below: *Lola Locket Liddle Kiddle, a Mattel design originating in 1967.*

spired by the famous Canadian quintuplets of that name. The transition to hard-plastic dolls in the early 1950s saw the advent of the seven-and-a-half-inch and eight-inch (19.1- and 20.3-cm) Storybook and International lines. Because most of the Alexander celebrity and character dolls were made from existing molds, it is hard to identify them without their original costumes, wigs, and wrist tags. The Cissette, Maggie, Margaret, and Lissy faces, to name only a few, have appeared on dozens of other character dolls over the decades. In 1967, the Marlo Thomas dolls from the T.V. show "That Girl" used the Elise face. There were rare exceptions, like the Shari Lewis head mold created for the 1959 doll of that name.

The Alexander Little Women sets of 1957-67 quickly became valuable collector's items. The dolls from Louisa May Alcott's children's classic were all hard plastic, with jointed knees and elbows. All used the Lissy face, with its rosebud closed mouth, sleep eyes, and saran wig, and were costumed in beautiful dresses of the Civil War era.

In 1960 the Pollyanna doll was produced under Disney

Right: *Skediddle Kiddle Shirley by Mattel and dating from the late 1960s.*

Below: *Mattel's Sweet Treat Kiddle from the 1960s and including a handy carrying case.*

Right: *Cheerful Tearful by Mattel from the 1960s.*

license to tie in with the movie about the engaging "glad girl." Pollyanna came in two sizes, 16 and 22 inches (41 and 65 cm) and was made of vinyl and plastic with rooted hair, sleep eyes with inset lashes, and open/closed mouth. She used the Kelly face, and wore a pink dress with black braid trim on the collar and hem, a straw hat decorated with flowers, and ribbon-tied pigtails.

The Alexander-kins line expanded to include many new dolls, including Wendy in a tennis outfit, and Wendy Ann in a two-piece felt dress. The delightful Maggie Mixup was a 1960 addition, available in both the eight-inch (20-cm) and 16½-inch (41.9-cm) sizes. She had straight red-orange hair with bangs, topped by a navy-and-white tam, and wore a white sweater and navy dress. Her green sleep eyes had inset lashes, her cheeks were freckled, and her mouth was closed and smiling. Like all the Alexander-kins dolls from 1953 to 1976, she was marked on the back "Alex". She was jointed at neck, shoulders, elbows, hips, knees, and ankles.

A lovely toddler doll named Caroline came out in 1961; she bore a striking resemblance to President John F. Kennedy's daughter. Caroline was vinyl and plastic and had rooted Saran hair with a side part, sleep eyes with inset lashes, and a smiling open/closed mouth. Fifteen inches (38 cm) tall, she was jointed at neck, shoulders, and hips, and wore a delicate lace-trimmed flower-print dress with white anklets, pink buttoned shoes with a strap, and "pearl" necklace and bracelet. Not coincidentally, the Jacqueline doll was introduced that same year, wearing an exact replica of Mrs. John F. Kennedy's elegant white satin inaugural ballgown with matching floor-length cape. The Jacqueline doll was 21 inches (53 cm) tall, made of vinyl and plastic, and had rooted hair, sleep eyes with inset lashes, smiling closed mouth, and high-heel feet. She was later used in the lovely 21-inch (53.3-cm) Portrait series as a figure from Gainsborough, Renoir, and *Godey's Ladies' Book*, as well as Agatha, Cornelia, Lady Hamilton, Magnolia, Melanie, and Mimi.

Far left: *Mattel's Bunson Burnie, from 1966-67. He is three inches tall with red hair and blue eyes. His accessory is a red fire truck, with a pair of removable white ladders.*

Left: *Babe Biddle, from the same period as Bunson Burnie, has brown hair and blue eyes. Her yellow plastic car has a red interior.*

Below left: *Maggie Mix-up by Madame Alexander, from the early years of the 1960s, was available in both eight-inch and 16½-inch sizes. The doll was jointed at the neck, shoulders, elbows, hips, knees, and ankles.*

International costumed dolls of the 1960s included Africa, American Girl, Amish Boy or Girl, Argentine Boy, Bolivia, Colonial Girl, Cowboy or Cowgirl, Easter Doll, Ecuador, and 11 others. The Cissette doll made a delightful Gibson Girl in 1962, joined the Gold Rush in 1963, took a page from *Godey's* in 1968, and appeared as Jenny Lind, "the Swedish Nightingale," in 1969. She was especially glamorous as Scarlett O'Hara, in the famous green velvet gown with bonnet to match.

Nineteen-sixty-six brought Coco, a fashionable 20-inch (51-cm) doll of vinyl and plastic, and the following year saw Nancy Drew, a 12-inch (31-cm) doll which would appear later in the character of Lord Fauntleroy. In 1965 Madame Alexander introduced Mary Ann, a 14-inch (36-cm) vinyl-and-plastic doll with a wistful expression, which was used for 10 different character dolls, including Goldilocks, Gidget, Poor Cinderella, and Orphan Annie. The Peter Pan set of 1969 included the famous flying boy along with Tinkerbell, Wendy, and Michael.

The Ideal Toy Corporation made great strides during the 1960s, beginning with the lifesize dolls of the Playpal series, which were the size of three-year-old children — up to 36 inches (91 cm) tall. Also called companion dolls, the Playpals and their imitators could wear real children's clothes and be posed in lifelike ways. They were all vinyl, with sleep eyes with inset lashes and closed mouths, jointed at neck, shoulders, and hips. They were marked

Above: *Amy, one of Madame Alexander's Little Women dolls manufactured from 1957 to 1967.*

Far left: *A selection of Madame Alexander's highly popular Little Women dolls based on the classic story by Louisa May Alcott. They are made in hard plastic and are jointed at elbows and knees.*

Left: *Meg, another of the Madame Alexander creations inspired by Louisa May Alcott's classic story.*

on the head "Ideal Doll, G-(#)," with the number corresponding to the doll's height, e.g., G-3. The dolls were named Patti, Penny, Peter, and Suzy, and Patti also came in a smaller 15-inch (38-cm) version, called Petite Patti. Other large dolls of the early 1960s were Miss Ideal and the Lori Martin doll, modeled on the child who starred in a remake of the Elizabeth Taylor classic movie *National Velvet*. She had long dark hair and wore a riding costume with checked shirt, stock, jeans, and boots. Miss Ideal came in two sizes: 25 and 30 inches (64 and 76 cm), and was vinyl and plastic with short rooted hair, sleep eyes with inset lashes, and a closed smiling mouth.

Betty Big Girl was a large (30-inch/76.2-cm) walking doll with a turning head and a battery-operated talking device. She had light green sleep eyes with lashes, and an open/closed mouth with molded teeth, and was made of plastic and vinyl.

Above: *Beth, like the other Little Women dolls, has the standard Lissy-mold face, with its distinctive rosebud closed mouth and sleepy eyes. All the dolls in the series were dressed in period costume.*

Right: *A Pollyanna doll, produced by Madame Alexander in the 1960s to promote the Walt Disney movie. She came in two sizes: 16 or 22 inches.*

Baby dolls remained an important part of the Ideal line. The original Betsy Wetsy doll became available in all vinyl, and Betsy Baby appeared in 1965. The lifelike Bye Bye Baby reached the market in 1960 in the 12-inch and 25-inch (30.5- and 61-cm) sizes. Kissy came in both Tiny and Baby versions, African-American and Caucasian,

Right: *Penny Brit, an eight-inch doll from the mid-1960s, produced by Deluxe.*

Far right: *Maggie Mix-up by Madame Alexander from 1960. The head is made from the Wand mold.*

Far left: *A show of affection for a Kissy doll, produced by Ideal. Kissy was available in Tiny and Baby versions.*

Left: *A doll of Lori Martin, who played Velvet in the television series "National Velvet," manufactured by the Ideal Toy Corporation. The head is made of vinyl.*

with a kissing action activated by pushing her stomach. These dolls were made of cloth and vinyl, like the Huggee Girl doll that Ideal sold from 1952. Goody Two Shoes was available in a walking and talking version almost as large as the Playpal dolls, while Tiny Boy, all plastic, was only eight inches (20 cm) high. He had sideways-looking blue sleep eyes and molded hair, with a one-piece head and body.

Several fashion dolls and doll families were introduced in response to Barbie. One which is quite rare now was the vinyl Jackie doll of the early 1960s, with high-heel feet and a variety of stylish outfits, including a green-and-red plaid suit with bolero jacket collared and cuffed in white, and a hat to match. The Tammy doll was produced from 1962 to 1966 and was advertised as "the doll you love to dress." She was 12 inches (30.5 cm) tall, and had a vinyl head and arms with plastic legs and torso. Her rooted saran hair was blonde or brunette, and she had painted side-glancing eyes and a closed mouth. Jointed at neck,

shoulders, and hips, she was held upright by a plastic stand that gripped her ankles. The original Tammy was dressed in a blue-and-white playsuit and white sneakers, and came with a style book that listed the outfits and accessories available.

In 1963 Tammy's family was introduced, including her little sister, Pepper, at nine-and-a-quarter inches (23 cm) tall. Pepper had a variety of costumes that were interchangeable with those of her friend Patti, introduced in 1964 as a Montgomery Ward exclusive. Similarly, Tammy's "mom" could wear many of the costumes designed for Tammy. Her "dad" and her brother, Ted, respectively 13 and 12½ inches (33 and 32 cm) tall, were much like Mattel's Ken doll, with Ted having brown painted eyes and light brown airbrushed hair. He, too, came packaged with a plastic stand and a style book.

A few years later, the nine-inch plastic-and-vinyl Jody doll, with bendable legs and floor-length hair, was introduced. The Crissy doll, with floor-length hair, came

Far left: *Ideal's answer to Barbie was Tammy, who was quick to acquire both family and friends. Seen here are her parents, brother Ted (left), little sister Pepper (front right), and Pepper's friend Patti (front left).*

Left: *Pebbles, daughter of the Flintstones cartoon family, is dressed prior to distribution to retail outlets by Ideal. These dolls were available in a plastic-vinyl mix or in vinyl alone.*

out in 1968 in an 18-inch (46-cm) version, and was produced with various features into the 1970s. Both dolls were similar to the Tressy doll, which came in both African-American and Caucasian models, in that their hair "grew" when a knob in the back was turned. Crissy had rooted auburn hair, dark brown sleep eyes with inset lashes, a smiling open/closed mouth with painted teeth; she was jointed at neck, shoulders, and hips.

The five-inch (32-cm) Flatsy was a novelty doll made of vinyl in a cutout style, which could be posed, not unlike a paper doll. There were nine dolls in the series (to 1970), each of which had rooted hair in psychedelic colors and painted features and came in a frame. An eight-inch (20-cm) Flatsy Fashion doll was produced in 1969.

Celebrity and character dolls remained a mainstay of the Ideal line throughout the 1960s. Shirley Temple dolls, in a variety of sizes and costumes, had never gone out of style, as the classic Temple movies like *Little Miss Marker* and *The Little Colonel* came to television. Parents who had loved the child star during the 1930s

were glad to meet the demand for the doll who brought back memories of their formative years. Ideal's flirty-eyed, all-vinyl Shirley Temple of the 1960s was extremely attractive; she came in a deluxe 17-inch (43-cm) version, with a lace-trimmed blue nylon dress with a pink ribbon sash.

Other Ideal character dolls of the 1960s included Pebbles and Bamm-Bamm, toddler dolls based on the Hanna Barbera cartoon series about the prehistoric Flintstone and Rubble families. These dolls were made in both plastic and vinyl and all vinyl. Pebbles wore two-piece rompers and a plastic bone in her topknot hairdo, and Bamm-Bamm was dressed in a leopard-print playsuit and cap, holding his own plastic bone in one hand. Both dolls had painted features and chubby cheeks, ragged-cut inset hair, and smiling mouths.

Ideal also produced a Samantha the Witch doll, modeled on the character played by Elizabeth Montgomery in the long-running television series "Bewitched." This 12-inch (30.5-cm) doll was of the

113

fashion-model type, made of vinyl and plastic, with high-heel feet. Samantha had green painted eyes glancing sideways or straight ahead, and long blonde rooted hair. She wore a floor-length sequined red dress slit to the knee in front, red high-heels, and a pointed red hat. She came with a plastic stand that gripped her at the waist.

Another durable television series spawned Ideal's "Beverly Hillbillies" set of 1963, which included a two-foot (61-cm) plastic car holding five characters from the show: Jed, Jethro, Elly May, Granny and Duke.

Horsman Dolls continued to produce imaginative and well-made dolls throughout the 1960s. Baby Buttercup was a lifelike baby doll made of soft vinyl with glassine sleep eyes. An open-mouth/nurser doll, she had either molded or rooted short hair, a "coo" voice box, tilting/turning head, and fully jointed body. Accessories for this doll included a nursing bottle, quilted blanket and/or lace-trimmed satin pillow, canopy cradle or ruffle-trimmed cradle with carrying handles, and a small pillow. Horseman's Baby Dribbles was created for a child to nurse back to health from a cold. She was 14 inches (35.6 cm) long, and came boxed with Kleenex tissues, a hot-water bag and thermometer, nursing bottle, pillow, and blanket. Made of vinyl and plastic, she had glassine sleep

eyes and rooted curly dark hair, an open mouth for nursing and holes in the nostrils for a running nose.

The soft vinyl Softee baby was African-American or Caucasian and ranged in size from 12 to 26 inches (30.5 to 66 cm). An open mouth/nurser, the doll had glassine sleep eyes and came with a nursing bottle and/or a canopy crib with blanket and pillow. Softee was also available as a boy-and-girl twin set, which, like the single dolls, was fully jointed, with rooted or molded hair, and a "coo" voice box. Many attractive baby clothes were available for Softee, including print and gingham dresses with ruffled bonnets or hairbows, and bootees.

For the burgeoning market in crying and wetting dolls, Horsman produced Tammy Tears, made of soft vinyl with glassine sleep eyes. Like the other Horsman baby dolls, she was available with both molded and rooted hair (dark or blonde), and was fully jointed. Her accessories included a nursing bottle and/or pacifier, washcloth, bib, sponge, soaps and a snap-lock suitcase with handle. Tynie Baby remained a popular member of the Horsman line, and could be purchased with a layette similar to the one for Tammy Tears.

At the expensive end of the Horsman line was a Walk-A-Bye Doll set, first offered as a three-piece unit in 1961.

Far left: *A Mary Poppins doll produced by the Horsman Doll Company in 1964 to help promote – and be promoted by – the film of the same name.*

Center left: *A Shirley Temple doll produced by the Ideal Toy Company in the 1960s. She is of all-vinyl construction and is 12 inches tall.*

Left: *Pebbles Flintstone and and Bamn-Bamm Rubble, both 12 inches tall, produced by Ideal.*

It included a companion-sized Princess Peggy walking doll, 36 inches (91 cm) tall, a folding baby carriage with canopy, and Baby Sister doll with molded hair and curved legs. The Princess Peggy doll was fully jointed, with tilting/turning head and rooted hair in short blonde curls.

Horsman produced its own Jackie doll in 1961, made of hard plastic with glassine sleep eyes and a closed mouth. She had slim legs with high-heeled feet, an adult body, and rooted curly dark hair. Jackie was taller than most of the fashion dolls – 20 and 25 inches (50.9 and 63.5 cm) – and came boxed with a flower-print sheath dress, high-heeled shoes, "pearl" necklace and earrings, and a hat. She was also sold as a bride doll, and other outfits and accessories were available.

Horsman's subteen, slim-legged Peggy Ann doll came in three sizes and was made of hard plastic with glassine sleep eyes, rooted hair, either blonde or dark, and a closed mouth. Fully jointed, she was available as a set with accessories variously titled Going Traveling, To the Prom, and Bride. Horsman's Ruthie doll, also made of hard plastic, came in both African-American and Caucasian versions, with a variety of costumes, including a nurse's uniform, pajamas and bathrobe, and short print dresses with hats to match. The Ruthie Goes Traveling

kit included several changes of clothing, a comb, a brush, a mirror, and several curlers. Horsman also continued to produce the popular Campbell Kids dolls, which it had been making since 1911, and others too numerous to mention.

Troll dolls were a phenomenon of the mid-1960s, and have recently made a comeback. They were made in sizes ranging from two-and-a-half to 10 inches (7 to 25.4 cm), with oversized ears, wide, flat noses, wrinkled foreheads, and large smiling mouths. Drawn from fairy tales about misshapen creatures who did mischief, the Troll dolls were unmistakably benign rather than menacing. Made of vinyl, they were jointed only at the neck, and had inset hair in wild colors like chartreuse and lavender, star-shaped hands with the fingers widely spread, short, stubby legs, and big, bare feet. Many Troll dolls were costumed, including the Scuba and Hawaiian Trolls, while others were characters, like the Santa Claus Trolls. There were also appealing Troll animals, including cows, donkeys, monkeys, turtles, and giraffes.

In the U.K., Pedigree Dolls and Toys Ltd. enjoyed great success with its Sindy doll, a Barbie-type teenage fashion doll with a wide array of clothes and accessories. Introduced in 1962, Sindy was 12 inches (30 cm) tall, with

Left: *One of the most popular types of doll from the 1960s – and beyond – was the Troll. They came in a variety of sizes.*

Right: *In response to the runaway success of Barbie, the English company, Pedigree, introduced Sindy in the early 1960s. She was 12 inches tall and had free-moving arms and legs. Here, Sindy is seen with Paul and Patch.*

free-moving arms and legs, and rooted hair that could be combed and styled. Sindy had a monopoly of the British market until 1980, and was the first doll to be advertised on television in the U.K.

Peggy Nisbet, of Somerset, England, has become very well known for her artistic costume dolls, including Queen Margaret of Scotland, Queen Eleanor of Aquitaine, Henry VIII and his wives, and Queen Berengaria, all produced during the 1960s. The future House of Nisbet began in 1953, when Peggy Nisbet designed a seven-inch (18-cm) model of Queen Elizabeth II to commemorate her coronation. The doll was made of fine bisque and dressed in coronation robes, with globe, scepter, and crown. It was limited to an edition of 250, all of which were sold by Harrods, the London department store. Over time, Peggy Nisbet made more than 600 other historical and national-costume dolls, using plastic, as well as storybook figures like Winnie the Pooh, Chris-

topher Robin, and Mary Poppins. In 1975 Jack Wilson became chairman and managing director of the House of Nisbet, and in 1989 it joined forces with R. Dakin Company, of San Francisco. Museum-quality Nisbet dolls of recent years include Prince Charles and Princess Diana, from the Royal Britannia Collection.

Beginning in 1966, one of the most popular dolls on the British market was the English-made Sasha. This vinyl doll with a body that could be posed, was produced in Stockport by the Friedland Doggart group, after designs by the Swiss doll artist Sasha Morgenthaler. She believed that a doll should have minimal facial modeling and expression so as to lend itself to the mood of the child playing with it. The Sasha dolls are comparable in quality to the expensive dolls produced by Käthe Kruse, but are much more affordable. The original Sasha dolls were 20 inches (51 cm) tall, and had wigs of natural hair, while the factory-produced models made in England under the

name Trendon are 16 inches (41 cm) tall and have rooted hair. Sasha Morgenthaler died in 1975, and her work is preserved in the museum of her name in Zurich. Her ideas on doll-making have had worldwide influence in terms of natural skin tones and authentic clothing for dolls depicting various nationalities.

The American Arranbee Doll Company had been acquired by the Vogue Doll Company in 1959, but the R. & B. mark was not discontinued until the early 1960s.

The Arranbee plastic-and-vinyl dolls were very well made, including Baby Marie, exclusive to the Kresge Stores. This doll had a plastic body with vinyl arms, legs, and head. She came with blue sleep eyes with molded lashes, excellent ear detailing, molded hair, and an open mouth for nursing. Baby Marie was dressed in a diaper, bootees, and bed jacket.

Another popular Arranbee doll of the 1960s was the 10-inch (25.4-cm) Littlest Angel, a toddler with a vinyl head and jointed knees for walking. The first doll in the Little Angel series had been produced in 1956, when Arranbee was best known for its Nancy Lee and Nanette dolls. Also continued from the 1950s was the plastic-and-vinyl My Angel doll, in sizes ranging from 17 to 22 inches (43.5 to 55.9 cm). My Angel had been available as a 30-inch (76.2-cm) walker unil 1959.

Arranbee also produced unmarked dolls to be dressed and sold by Mollye (Marysia) Goldman of the Inter-

national Doll Company and Hollywood Cinema Fashions. Mollye, in turn, designed clothes for many other dollmakers, including Horsman, Ideal, and Eegee (Goldberger). She had emigrated from Russia with her family as a small child and became a skillful seamstress at an early age. After her marriage to Myer Goldman in 1919, she began making commercial dolls and dolls' clothing. Mollye was the first to offer a set of Little Women dolls, and she dressed Shirley Temple dolls, including

Left: *G.I. Joe (a registered trademark of Hasbro, Inc. All rights reserved) was one of the few dolls successfully aimed at young boys. He made his debut in 1964.*

Right: *Heidi, by Remco, was introduced in 1965. The company also produced many character dolls based on popular television series, such as "I Dream of Jeannie" and "Orphan Annie."*

Far left: *A selection of Arranbee's Littlest Angel Dolls of different decades. From left to right: the 1950s, 1960s and 1970s.*

Left: *Heidi and Winking Heidi by Remco Toys. Winking Heidi was introduced in 1968; Heidi, three years earlier.*

those made by Ideal (to 1936). Her own Hollywood Cinema Fashions produced many movie-star dolls, including Jeanette McDonald, Ginger Rogers, and Judy Garland.

Remco made a variety of character and baby dolls during the 1960s. In 1963 it produced the Littlechap Family, which bore a close resemblance to the John F. Kennedy family. These four plastic dolls ranged in size from the 14½-inch (36.5-cm) Dr. John to the 10½-inch (26.5-cm) Libby. The mother, Lisa, was 13½ inches tall and wore a "fur" coat and hat over a sheath dress, blue eye shadow, and gold earrings. Judy, the older daughter, wore a red coat, white gloves, "pearl" earrings, and a leopard-print hat and scarf. The smallest doll, Libby, was dressed in a black-and-red plaid coat with a red head scarf, gloves, and purse, while Dr. John had a stylish blue trench coat and a fedora. Other Remco dolls of the period included Heidi (1965) and Winking Heidi (1968), Baby Sad or Glad (1966), Baby Crawlalong (1967), Baby Grow a Tooth, and Baby Know it All (both 1969). Remco character dolls based on media personalities included the Addams Family, I Dream of Jeannie, and Orphan Annie.

Deluxe Topper became very well known for its bat-tery-operated and other "dolls that did things" during the 1960s. These included Baby Catch A Ball, Baby Peek 'N' Play, Li'l Miss Fussy, and Smarty Pants. Dolls of the Topper Toys Go-Go series had one-piece bodies and limbs with wire so that they could be posed freely, including Private Ida, which came in a detective's trench coat and hat. Deluxe also continued to make more traditional dolls, like the eight-inch (20.3-cm) Penny Brite, which has become highly collectable.

Hasbro, Inc., which had been in the toy and doll business since 1922, made history and anticipated the 1970s with its G.I. Joe action-figure doll, introduced in 1964. Made of vinyl and plastic, G.I. Joe had molded hair, painted black, brown, or blond (an African-American soldier was added the following year), painted eyes, and a closed mouth. He was indeed an action figure, as he was joined at neck, shoulders, upper arms, elbows, wrists, waist, hips, knees, and ankles. Until 1967, when his patent number was added, he was marked on the right hip "G.I. Joe/Copyright 1964/by Hasbro/Patent Pending/Made in U.S.A." The first G.I. Joe doll had a scar on his face, which did not appear on the Talking Commander model introduced in 1967.

CHAPTER FIVE

A World of Dolls

Left: *Mattel's Live Action Barbie, dressed for the disco, appeared at the beginning of the 1970s.*

Above: *Although this particular doll, Victoria Plum, dates from the 1980s, she is indicative of the movement toward dolls based on TV programmes, movies and children's books that gathered momentum in the 1970s.*

Action figures – many of them based on characters from the media – came into their own in the 1970s. Manufacturers focused on realism and mobility, and their models were as diverse as G.I. Joe and the robots and aliens of the *Star Wars* motion pictures. Cartoon characters, television personalities, and comic-book heroes all had their day in the sun. At the same time, baby dolls, fashion dolls, costume dolls, and other traditional playthings, retained their hold on children's hearts.

In 1966 Hasbro had followed up its successful G.I. Joe #1 with a set of six soldiers from other armies, including the British, Australian, French, German, Japanese, and Soviet. (None of them had the facial scar of the original.) By 1970 there were nine models in the G.I. Joe #4 series, which all had flocked hair, and some had beards. Many accessories became available with such sets as Land Adventurer, Sea Adventurer, Air Adventurer, and Astronaut.

By mid-decade, G.I. Joe had diversified into new fields, with sets including Fire Fighter, Military Police-

man, Ski Patrol, Secret Agent, Nurse, Frogman, and Green Beret, the latter representing the Special Forces created during the Vietnam War. Accessories included an armored car, a motorcycle with sidecar (by Irwin, which had made Barbie's first sportscar), space capsule, sea sled, tank, jeep, helicopter, and all-terrain vehicle (A.T.V.). As public sentiment turned against militarism as a result of the Vietnam experience, G.I. Joe became more of an adventurer than a fighting man, as is seen in such sets as Safari, Test Pilot, Jungle Explorer, Polar Explorer, and Space Man.

A very unusual Hasbro doll of the early 1970s was Leggie, available in both African-American and Caucasian versions. These 10-inch (25.4-cm) dolls were all vinyl, with painted features and very long, bendable legs. Dressed in colorful, trendy clothes, they were marked "Hasbro/1972/HK."

Hasbro also produced a set of "Charlie's Angels" dolls, modeled on the three female stars of the popular 1970s television adventure series: Kelly (Jaclyn Smith),

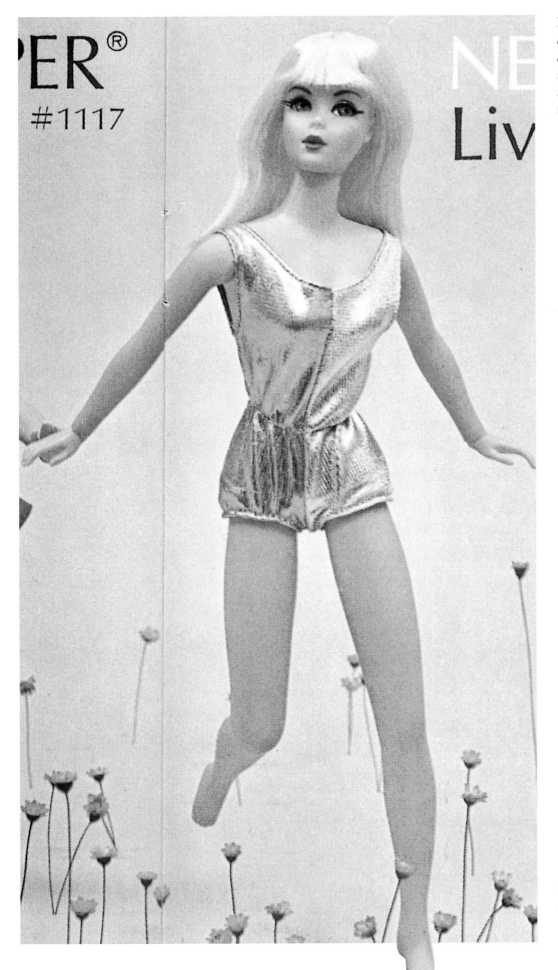

#1117

Far left: *The growth in accessories during the 1960s and 1970s is clearly indicated by the picture of this youngster taking tea with a Tracy doll.*

Left: *A 1970 Living Barbie. As women gained more freedom during the 1970s, Barbie moved with the times.*

Left: *An obviously popular series of doll created to tie in with a popular T.V. series and later movies. These Star Trek dolls comprise Dr. McCoy, Captain Kirk, Spock and Scotty.*

Above: *A Klingon, one of the* Enterprise's *most dangerous foes in the Star Trek stories.*

Right: *An alien figure from the Star Trek doll series.*

Center right: *A Star Trek doll more likely to female members of the program – communications expert Lieutenant Uhuru.*

Far right: *Another alien against whom the Star Trek heroes could do battle.*

Sabrina (Kate Jackson), and Jill (Farrah Fawcett-Majors). These eight-and-a-half-inch (21.5-cm) dolls were licensed by Spelling-Goldberg Productions and advertised as "The Beautiful Girls Who Live Dangerously."

Kenner Products Inc., then a subsidiary of General Mills, began to make action figures based on the movie *Star Wars* in 1974. The demand for characters and accessories from this science-fiction movie was almost unprecedented, and Kenner enjoyed great success with its *Star Wars* "Large Set" (1978-80). The dolls which had human faces were all vinyl with molded and painted hair (except for Princess Leia, who had rooted hair), painted features, and bodies jointed at neck, shoulders, and hips. The other figures were fully jointed and made of styrene. The set consisted of Princess Leia and Luke Skywalker, both 11 inches (27.9 cm) high; Chewbacca and Darth

Vader, 15 inches (39.1 cm) high; the robots C3PO and R2D2, respectively 12 and seven inches (30.5 and 17.8 cm); Han Solo, 12 inches (30.5 cm) high; and five other characters from *Star Wars* and its sequels, *The Empire Strikes Back* and *Return of the Jedi.*

Other Kenner action figures of the 1970s included the science-fiction-inspired Six Million Dollar Man and Bionic Woman, both generated by television series. These 13- and 12-inch (33- and 30.5-cm) dolls had extra joints and painted features, the man had molded hair and the woman (modeled on actress Jamie Sommers) had long blonde, rooted hair.

Another set of action figures made by Mego Corporation evolved from the popular television series "Star Trek" during the late 1960s. The characters included Mr. Spock, Dr. McCoy, Lt. Uhura, a Klingon, Scotty,

Heroes" series. There was also an "Arch Enemy" series featuring adversaries of the super heroes, including Penguin, Joker, Riddler, and Mr. Mxyzptlk.

In 1974 Mego came out with the Greatest Super Gals series, including Wonder Woman, Super Girl, Bat Girl, and Cat Woman. The Wild West was not neglected: Wyatt Earp, Cochise, Davy Crockett, Buffalo Bill Cody, Wild Bill Hickok, and Sitting Bull proved the enduring fascination to children of cowboys and Indians. Other Mego dolls represented popular entertainment personalities like Cher, Diana Ross, and Joe Namath, all 12 inches (30.5 cm) tall, with extra joints at wrists, elbows, waist, knees, and ankles.

Mattel's Barbie, the queen of the fashion dolls, retained her popularity throughout the 1970s, at home and abroad. Barbie sets of the decade included Growing Pretty Hair, Quick Curl, Newport, Sun Valley, Sweet Sixteen, Funtime, and Ballerina. In 1976 Gold Medal Barbie (*Medaille d'Or Barbie*) in French Canada) took part in the Olympic Games. Super Size Barbie, 18 inches (46 cm) tall, was introduced the same year. She was

and Captain Kirk. The male figures wore black-collared uniform shirts in red, blue, and gold, with gold-braided cuffs, and black pants and boots. They had painted features and molded hair and carried ray guns. Many other toys and accessories were inspired by "Star Trek," which was just as popular in the U.K. as it was in the United States. The release of several *Star Trek* movies beginning in 1979, saw the continuance of the Star Trek phenomenon into the 1980s.

Mego also produced many other eight-inch (20.3-cm) action figures based on television and movie series, all marked on the shoulder blades "© Mego Corp./year date (Rom. numerals)." Those of the early and mid-1970s included Action Jackson, Superman, Batman, Robin, Aquaman, Captain America, Tarzan, Spider Man, and Shazam – collectively, the "World's Greatest Super

Far left: *A Kestner doll, measuring 31 inches, from the 1970s. She has a ball-jointed, composition body, a bisque head with brown glass eyes, and a blonde wig. The teddy bear was made by Steiff.*

Left: *A child pictured holding a telephone conversation with a talking Hi Diottie doll, produced by Mattel. The doll had a range of 12 different phrases which were activated at random by squeezing the hand set.*

Page 132: *A pair of dolls created by Mattel as part of a series to celebrate the American Bicentennial. These two are dressed as a Southern belle and a colonial lady.*

Page 133: *Another pair of Bicentennial dolls commemorating the early pilgrims who settled along the Eastern seaboard of the United States.*

plastic and vinyl with rooted hair, jointed waist, painted features, and a stand. Her outfits could be purchased separately.

By this time, Barbie accessories included a roadster, sportscar, dune buggy, clock, house, airplane, horse (Dancer), and wardrobe chest. No other fashion doll had come close. Deluxe Topper entered the field in 1970 with the very attractive Dawn Model Agency series, including the six-inch (15.2-cm) Dawn, Daphne, and Dinah. The colorful packaging for these dolls showed them in elegant fashion-model settings that co-ordinated with their outfits, including a red-and-gold short-skirted playsuit, a floor-length pink-and-white ballgown trimmed with ruffles at bodice and hem, and a strapless silver-and-green metallic gown with an oversized hair bow. There was a

companion set called Boys of Dawn, comparable to the Ken doll from Mattel but proportionally smaller.

Ideal offered the 12-inch (30.5-cm) Tuesday Taylor fashion doll and her boyfriend Eric, successors to the Crissy and Tammy families. However, baby and child dolls remained more prominent in Ideal's line. The all-vinyl Baby Crissy (1972) came in both African-American and Caucasian models, with "grow hair" and a pull-string talking device. The finger and toe detail on this doll was excellent, as it was on Ideal's seven-inch (17.8-cm) Baby, Baby of 1974. Made of heavy vinyl, with a one-piece body and limbs, Baby, Baby had inset blue eyes with molded lashes and an open mouth for nursing. When the bottle was inserted into her mouth, her cheeks sank in like those of a feeding baby.

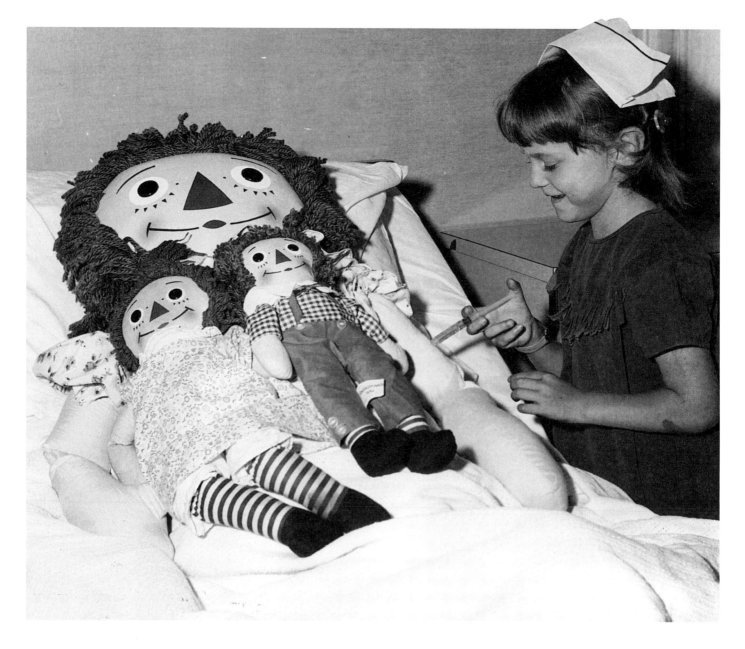

Ideal was among the first American manufacturers to produce anatomically correct or "sexed" dolls, including the Joey Stivic doll, modeled on the grandson of Archie Bunker in the television series "All in the Family." This 15-inch (38.1-cm) doll was all vinyl, with a one-piece body and limbs, painted blue eyes, and open mouth for nursing.

Mattel produced a sexed girl doll made of plastic and vinyl with a protruding upper lip and blue sleep eyes with lashes. She had rooted blonde hair and lifelike hands and feet and was made at the Ratti factory in Italy after it was purchased by Mattel. Baby Brother Tenderlove was another sexed doll from Mattel. He had a one-piece Dublon body and a vinyl head with decal brown eyes. Like Ideal's Joey Stivic, he was an open-mouthed nursing doll. Mattel also enjoyed great success with Baby Thataway, a battery-operated doll with jointed knees that crawled and walked. Made of plastic, with a vinyl head, she had

painted brown sideways-glancing eyes, a closed mouth, and curly rooted hair. She was first produced in 1974.

An appealing cloth doll with a vinyl head was Mattel's Mama Beans, who came with tiny twins (the Baby Beans) in matching bonnets. All three were dressed in a floral print, and Mama had rooted hair pulled back into a bun, and a stitched-on bonnet. The twins had vinyl heads with five painted curls on the forehead. Mattel's Honey Hill Bunch featured cloth dolls with vinyl heads and painted features, most about six inches (15.2 cm) tall. The freckled Hayseed doll was dressed like a farm boy and came with Chum, a felt-and-plush dog with a vinyl head and velour strips on his back to hold Hayseed.

Another novelty doll of the 1970s was Kenner's Blythe, which had a small body and an oversize head. She was 12 inches (30.5 cm) tall, made of vinyl and plastic, and had a pull string that made her eyes change color and position.

Left: *A doll of Bert, one of the characters in Sesame Street, meets a young fan.*

The engaging Kewpie doll had been on the scene since 1909, when she was created by illustrator Rose O'Neill for the *Ladies' Home Companion*. The original Kewpie dolls were manufactured in Germany, but eventually the Cameo Doll Company was formed to make them in the United States. Since then they have been licensed to several dollmakers, including Knickerbocker and Jesco. Kewpies have been made of bisque, composition, Celluloid, cloth, plastic, and vinyl, but all have large, sideways-glancing eyes, closed, smiling mouths, chubby cheeks, and the famous Kewpie curl and topknot. During the early 1970s, Cameo produced the four-inch (10.2-cm) vinyl Kewpie Thinker, with its chin resting on its hands and its elbows on its knees. There was also a Kewpie with a bean-bag-type body, and the more traditional all-vinyl Kewpie jointed at neck, shoulders, and hips, and dressed in rompers or a baby smock with ruffled pants to match. Kreuger made a Kewpie 12 inches (30.5 cm) tall,

and Montgomery Ward's department store made an eight-inch (20.5-cm) doll for its 1972 anniversary.

Knickerbocker Toys, long known for its storybook and character dolls, enjoyed great success during the 1970s with its Holly Hobbie series, licensed by American Greeting Cards. These six-and-a-half-inch to 10-inch (16.5- to 25.4-cm) old-fashioned dolls were made of vinyl, or plastic and vinyl, and wore sunbonnets, gingham dresses, and high-top or strapped shoes with long stockings. The series included Carrie, with freckles and brown painted eyes; Amy, with freckles and blue painted eyes; and Holly Hobbie, with a round face, light freckles, and painted brown eyes, wearing a patchwork apron. They were all fully jointed, with removable clothes, and could be purchased with accessories including a baby carriage, toy cat, watering can, wagon, and potted plants. In the same mode, Knickerbocker produced its own line of Sunbonnet Dolls, including Mandy, May, and Molly. An-

Left: *An English example of the postwar doll diversity. This example – Sasha – was made by Trendon of Stockport in the early 1970s.*

Right: *Joey, a character from the Archic Bunker T.V. shows, dates from the 1970s.*

other set was inspired by the long-running television series "The Little House on the Prairie," based on the novels of Laura Ingalls Wilder.

The U.S. Bicentennial in 1976 saw many commemorative dolls from American history. The Mattel series included the Prairie Settler, Southern Belle, Pilgrim Couple, Indian Girl, and Colonial Lady. Madame Alexander initiated her First Lady series with Set I – six dolls representing Martha Washington, Abigail Adams, Martha Randolph, Dolley Madison, Elizabeth Monroe, and Louisa Adams. These beautifully costumed dolls used the Mary Ann and Martha faces and were made of vinyl and plastic. They had sleep eyes with inset lashes, rooted hair, and closed mouths, and were jointed at neck, shoulders, and hips. All the dolls in this series were 14 inches (36 cm) tall. In 1979 Set II went into production, consisting of Sarah Jackson, Angelica Van Buren, Jane Findlay, Julia Tyler, Sarah Polk, and Betty Taylor Bliss.

Beginning in 1965, Madame Alexander made several sets of seven dolls representing the characters from the movie *The Sound of Music*. The large set (1965-70) used an Elise-faced doll for Maria; Mary Ann-faced dolls for

Brigitta, Liesl, and Louisa; and Janie-faced dolls for Friedrich, Gretl, and Marta. These dolls ranged in size from 17 inches (43 cm) to 11 inches (28 cm). The small "Sound of Music" set ranged in size from the 12-inch (31-cm) Marie, to the eight-inch (20-cm) Friedrich, Gretl, and Marta. Maria had a Nancy Drew face, and the Cissette face was used for Brigitta, Liesl, and Louisa.

At about this time, Welsh designer Odette Aiden was making a handsome series of historical dolls in plastic, with painted features, jointed at the shoulders and wearing costumes faithful to their eras. These seven-and-a-half- to eight-and-a-half-inch (19.1- to 21.5-cm) dolls included Mary Queen of Scots, Jane Seymour, Anne Boleyn, Lady Hamilton, Queen Elizabeth II, and the Prince of Wales at his 1969 investiture at Caernarvon Castle. In England, the beautiful Old Cottage Dolls recalled a gracious era, with their straw bonnets, hoops and baskets. They had all-felt bodies and composition swivel heads with painted features. Their hands were mitt-style, with freestanding thumbs.

In 1972 Ideal reprised its classic Shirley Temple doll in the 17 inch (43 cm) size. She was made of vinyl and

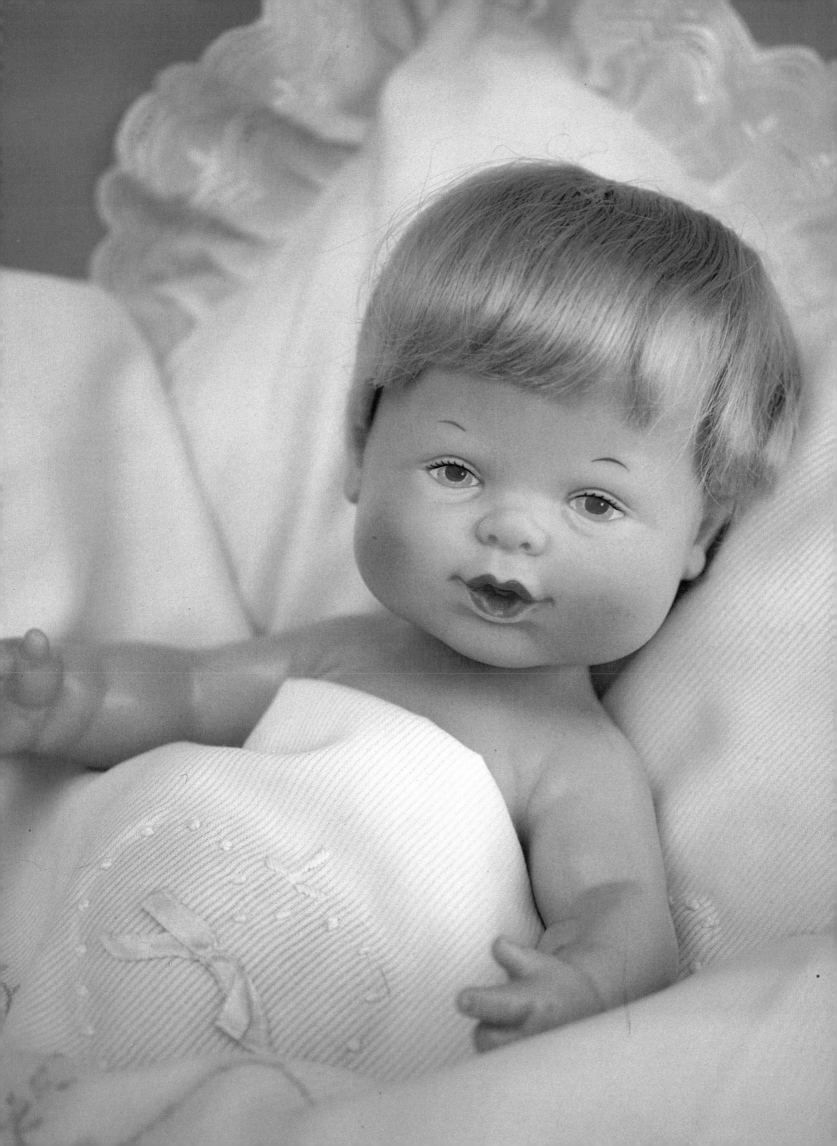

Above: A classic example of doll longevity. This picture was taken in 1974 as part of the Kewpie doll's sixtieth birthday celebrations.

Effanbee had built its reputation on beautiful composition dolls like Honey and the Lovums baby doll, so it was not surprising that it returned to that material for its Limited Edition Doll Club, designed for collectors. Limited Edition dolls of the period between 1975 and 1979 included Precious Baby, Patsy, Crowning Glory, and Skippy, an old-fashioned boy doll with a double-breasted brown coat and cap, a black-and-white over-sized bow tie, and black lace-up shoes. Doll artist Dewees Cochran designed the club's 1977 offering.

Vogue Doll's delightful Ginny dolls, in production since the late 1940s, generated the Ginny Doll Club in 1973. Ginny and family had appeared as storybook characters like Hansel and Gretel; costume dolls, including brides, majorettes, and clowns; and children of other countries (the Far-Away Lands series). In 1972 the all-vinyl Ginny "Africa" was introduced: an eight-inch (20.3-cm) brown-skinned doll with amber eyes and an Afro hairstyle, dressed in a dashiki and wearing gold jewelry. That same year, Vogue's Ginny Set #1000 came to market with an eight-inch (20.3-cm) toddler doll, made of plastic with a vinyl head, sleep blue eyes, and molded lashes. She wore a short jumper and a long-sleeved blouse and also had two extra outfits. This doll was marked on the head "Ginny," and on the back "Vogue Dolls 1972/Made in Hong Kong." Another attractive doll of this period was Little Miss Ginny, who wore a pink knitted dress with white cotton sleeves and an embroidered band on the skirt. She was 12 inches (30.5 cm) tall, made of plastic and vinyl, and marked on the head "Vogue."

During the mid-1970s, Vogue was sold to Lesney of England, which continued to make dolls tagged "Vogue" until it sold the molds to Tonka Toys, Inc. Lesney-era dolls include the 16-inch (40.6-cm) Brickette doll, of plastic and vinyl with sleep eyes and a "mod" hairdo in tight red curls. This doll wore a rust-red pinafore over a black-and-rust floral print dress with ruffled sleeves and hem, long white stockings, and black-and-white shoes. She was marked on the head "Lesney Prod. Corp. 1978/71679" and her dress was tagged "Vogue Dolls, Inc." (Lesney was best known in the United States as the maker of the Matchbox line of miniature cars and trucks.)

Another popular Vogue doll continued by Lesney was the Littlest Angel, a toddler doll of plastic and vinyl with sleep eyes, snub nose, and closed smiling mouth. One 15-inch (38.1-cm) version came with orange-red hair in side ponytails tied with yellow ribbon, and wore a striped turtleneck shirt and overalls. The Littlest Angel dolls had been manufactured since 1950, beginning with the Arran-bee Doll Company, before it was acquired by Vogue.

Horsman Dolls brought many of its classic baby and toddler dolls, including Baby Buttercup, into the 1970s, when several new dolls were added to the line as well. The 12-inch (30.5-cm) Baby Dumpling doll had a foam-

plastic, and had inset eyes and lashes, a smiling mouth with teeth, and joints at neck, shoulders, and hips. The Danbury Mint made a collector's 14-inch (35.6-cm) Shirley Temple doll in porcelain with glass eyes and auburn sausage curls, dressed in a Scottish outfit and valued at well over $300 at the time of writing.

Effanbee designed a Bicentennial Boy and Girl doll (Pun'kin) in the mode of its American Children series – a line of composition dolls of the 1930s and 1940s. Portrait dolls of George and Martha Washington and Betsy Ross were also produced in 1976. The company made a series of Disney dolls in 1977-78, including Cinderella, Snow White, Alice in Wonderland, and Sleeping Beauty, all 14 inches (35.6 cm) tall.

filled body, a vinyl head and limbs, painted eyes, and a closed mouth. Her features were chubby, her arms and legs bent, and her rooted blonde hair was either straight or curled. She came with a satin-trimmed blanket and a short dress trimmed at the neck with lace and a bow. Baby Sharon came as an African-American or a Caucasian and had either glassine sleep eyes or painted eyes. She was an open-mouthed drinking and wetting doll with infant features, bent arms and legs, and molded or rooted hair in black or blonde. Accessories included a quilted bunting or a satin-trimmed blanket and a nursing bottle.

Baby Tweaks was an 18-inch (46-cm) African-American or Caucasian doll with a "coo" voice box activated by squeezing her foam-filled body. Her head, arms and legs were vinyl, and she had glassine eyes and a closed smiling mouth.

Horsman toddler dolls included the 21-inch (53.3-cm) Drinkee Walker doll, with full-sized baby bottle, which walked, drank, and wet. She was made entirely of vinyl and had glassine sleep eyes, an open mouth, and rooted hair, either blonde or black. The smaller-size vinyl Drinkee Baby also came as an African-American or Caucasian, and was fully jointed. Eleven inches (27.9 cm) tall, she came with a layette including several changes of clothing, a nursing bottle, comb, brush, and mirror.

Thirstee Walker, 26 inches (66 cm) tall, was Horsman's largest toddler doll – a very lifelike child doll with drinking, wetting, and walking features. She was available as an African-American or Caucasian model, was made of vinyl and fully jointed, and had glassine sleep eyes and rooted blonde or black hair. Teenie Bopper was a smaller toddler doll (11 inches/27.9 cm high), with painted eyes and an open or closed mouth. She wore a short-sleeved two-piece dress with buttons down the front, anklets, strapped shoes, and a hair bow.

An unusual novelty doll of the early 1970s was Horsman's Peggy Pen-Pal, a fully jointed 18-inch (46-cm) toddler doll which came with a two-sided desk. Her movable arms were activated by drawing or writing on the opposite side of the desk, which had two pens and several writing pads. Horsman's walking Ruthie doll remained available in several sizes, with large, painted sideways-glancing eyes and an open/closed mouth. She was either African-American or Caucasian, and was made entirely of vinyl. Pooty Tat was an engaging nine-inch (22.9-cm) doll – boy and girl – which came in striped pajamas with pompons down the front and a striped nightcap. This doll had sleep eyes, an open or closed mouth, and a rounded stomach. It was made of vinyl and fully jointed.

Sound-making dolls retained their popularity, and Horsman made numerous dolls of this type. One was Musical Lullabye Baby, which twisted and turned when her music box was activated by a pull string. She was 12 inches (30.5 cm) tall, with painted eyes, rooted hair, and

an open mouth for nursing. The Tynie Baby line had a "coo" sound voice box, and the 18-inch (46-cm) New Arrival doll had a "Mama" voice box. She had a vinyl head, arms, and legs, and a foam-filled body. The 16-inch (40.6-cm) "Mama" Baby was very similar, with bent legs and arms and rooted hair.

R. John Wright Dolls was founded by John and Susan Wright during the 1970s to make artistic cloth dolls. They first made a series of character old men and women, comparable in quality to the dolls of Lenci, Steiff, and Käthe Kruse. Later they concentrated on child dolls, including Arthur and Lilian, modeled on their son and daughter. Both the Wrights are involved in the many stages of sophisticated doll-making, including scale drawing, sculpting in clay, and handpainting of features. Their loveliest creations include characters from classic children's books, including Christopher Robin, Red Riding Hood, and The Little Prince.

Britain's Helene McLeod, a member of the British Dollmaker's Association, has become well known for her finely made stuffed cloth playdolls with latex heads covered with stockinet. Ms. McLeod is a world traveler who spent almost two decades in various parts of Africa. Some of her most attractive ethnic dolls are of African and Asian children.

English doll artist Vina Cooke experimented with doll-making as a child and continued after her daughter was born, making cloth dolls with painted faces. They were well received, and she perfected her techniques, discovering a talent for portraiture. Working only with cloth, wire, stuffing, and glue, she has made such portrait dolls as Prince William and other personalities, which have found their way into many collections. Another noteworthy English doll artist is Charlotte Zeepvat, who specializes in historical figures made from old photographs in the medium of air-hardening clay. One of her portrait groups – Queen Mary with her second son, later George VI – is on display at Windsor Castle.

Many changes occurred in the doll-making world during the 1970s. One of the most significant was the increased importance placed on packaging. Where dolls had once come to market in a simple box marked with a name and a stock number, the emphasis shifted to colorful, modern, well-designed packaging, which could cost as much as the doll itself. Concurrently, the description "Mint in Box" became more important to collectors, and the condition of both doll and package became a greater determinant of value. New doll artists, producing limited editions, came to the fore, and collectors became both more numerous and more specialized, concentrating on, say, celebrity dolls, and even on specific celebrities like Shirley Temple or Judy Garland, and other kinds of memorabilia associated with them. There was also a growing trend toward making dolls from kits and molds.

CHAPTER SIX

Dolls of Today

Left: *A pair of Cabbage Patch Kids dolls, the success story of the 1980s. They are manufactured by Coleco, originally known as the Connecticut Leather Company.*

Above: *Following on from the Star Trek dolls seen in the last chapter, here is one of the heroes of the* Star Wars *movie trilogy – Princess Leia.*

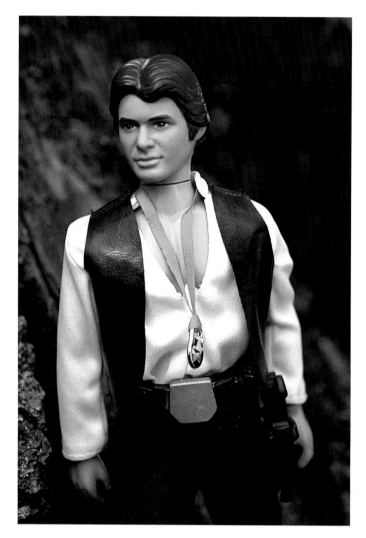

The last few decades of the twentieth century have brought many innovations in doll-making. Celebrity dolls – some of them extremely expensive – have soared to new heights of popularity. Since 1983, more than 250 new celebrity dolls have been manufactured; they include faithful likenesses of movie and sports personalities, military heroes, politicians, royalty, and figures from history.

In 1983 World Doll began to produce its celebrity series, starting with Marilyn Monroe, a beautifully packaged 18½-inch (47-cm) vinyl doll with rooted platinum-blonde hair, painted blue eyes, an open/closed mouth with molded teeth, and a painted "beauty spot" on the cheek. She wore a floor-length fitted red gown and a white feather boa, and was designed by Joyce Christopher. That same year, World Doll produced an all-porcelain Marilyn Monroe by the same designer, dressed in a silver mesh gown, a floor-length white mink coat, and diamond earrings and necklace. It retailed for $6,500.

The British royal family has been the subject of doll-makers from Madame Alexander to the House of Nisbet, resulting in likenesses of Queen Elizabeth II, Prince Charles, Princess Diana, the Queen Mother, Princess Anne as a bride, Prince Philip, and Prince William, among others. In 1980 Effanbee began producing its Legend Series of vinyl dolls, with W.C. Fields and Mae West.

Doll designers like Lee Middleton have found a ready market for their sculpted portrait dolls, many of them modeled from life. Middleton began making portrait dolls in porcelain bisque in 1978. Demand was so great that

she moved into the medium of porcelain-like vinyl in 1980, working with her sister Sharon Wells, who designed the dolls' clothing. Her First Moments series includes the beautiful 21-inch (53.5-cm) Christening Doll, with vinyl head, hands, and feet and a cloth torso, painted features, and an heirloom christening gown and bonnet trimmed with lace and ribbons. Like all Middleton's dolls, this sleeping baby comes with a tiny Bible.

Above, far left: *Han Solo, one of the dolls created to promote the* Star Wars *films.*

Above: *Barbie's continuing popularity is reflected in this display of dolls.*

Overleaf: *A display of dolls styled to represent notable English personalities, including Prince Charles and Princess Diana, as well as Winston Churchill and King Henry VIII.*

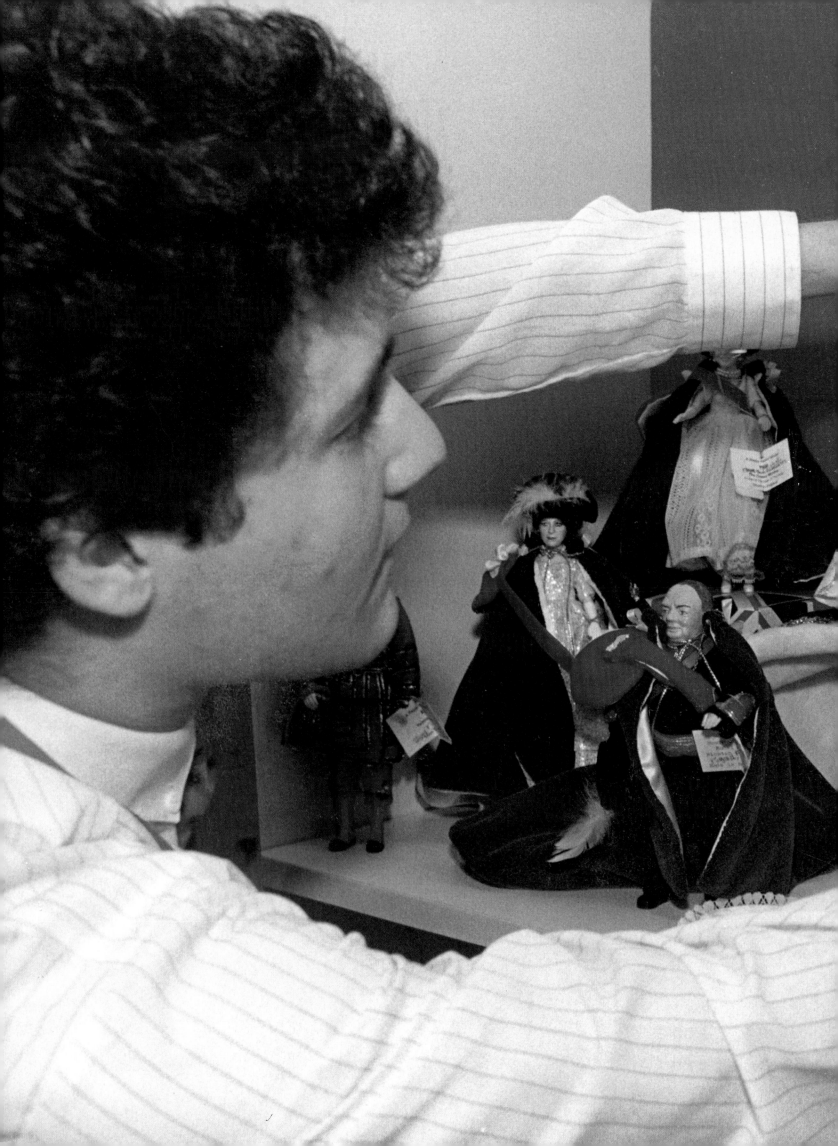

The Franklin Mint has been producing elegant portrait dolls in traditional materials – bisque shoulders, heads and limbs on cloth bodies – since 1987. Its Heirloom Doll series includes the Gibson Bride, Rapunzel, Disney's Snow White, Swan Lake, and Scarlett O'Hara.

Doll designer Robin Woods became well known in the 1980s for her lovely limited-edition dolls and accessories, including the 14-inch (35.6-cm) Merri, Mindy, Angelina, and Noelle, the latter two being Christmas angels made for J.C. Penneys. In 1992 Woods became the creative designer for the Alexander Doll Company, succeeding Madame Beatrice Alexander, who had died in 1990. Fortunately, to celebrate her sixty-first year as a dollmaker in 1984, Madame Alexander consented to the production of a likeness of herself – a 21-inch (53.3-cm) elegantly gowned, all-vinyl doll, with blonde rooted hair and brown sleep eyes. It was an appropriate tribute to a woman who had become a legend in the world of dolls.

New names emerged during the 1980s, including Galoob, which became known for its action-figure sets like The A-Team, Soldiers of Fortune, based on a

Below: *Not the real thing! These bogus Cabbage Patch Kids dolls were seized by U.S. customs in Baltimore, and were imported from Taiwan.*

Right: *Real Cabbage Patch Kids dolls with their creator, Xavier Roberts, September 1987.*

television adventure series. The best-known member of the team was burly Mr. T – Lawrence Tureaud – who played the menacing B.A. Baracus, a mechanical genius. Galoob's Mr. T wears his trademark heavy gold chains, earrings, bracelets, and rings, and high-top sneakers. Later, Galoob diversified its line with the character Baby Face Doll series, made of vinyl and jointed at neck, shoulder, hips, elbows, and knees. Tomy made an impact in 1984 with its attractive Kimberly doll, available in both African-American and Caucasian versions with a closed or smiling mouth. The original Gettin' Fancy Kimberly was a well-made set comprising a 16-inch (40.6-cm) vinyl doll with rooted hair and painted features, for which additional clothes could be purchased separately: soccer, roller-skating, ice-skating, party, and school outfits,

jeans, and others. The doll was made in Hong Kong and the clothes in China. It retailed for $24.95.

The runaway success story of the 1980s was, of course, the Cabbage Patch Kids dolls from Coleco, originally the Connecticut Leather Company, founded by Maurice Greenberg in 1932. In 1982 his son, Arnold Greenberg, secured the licensing rights to the "Little People" handmade cloth dolls created by Xavier Roberts in 1977. Coleco introduced its renamed versions of Roberts' dolls in June 1983, hoping to sell perhaps a million of them by Christmas. The Cabbage Patch Kids dolls set off an unprecedented surge of buying and media attention that resulted in sales of 2.5 million by year's end, with hundreds of thousands of back orders still unfilled.

Above left: *A pair of Cabbage Patch Kids dolls manufactured by Hasbro.*

The original Cabbage Patch Kid was a 16-inch (40.6-cm) vinyl-headed doll with rooted yarn hair, decal eyes, closed or open/closed mouth (some with one or two dimples), a receding chin, and a cloth body, arms, and legs. These dolls were marked on the head "Copy R. 1978 1982/Original Appalachian Art Works Inc./Manufactured by Coleco Ind. Inc." and on the left buttock with the signature of Xavier Roberts and the year date "'85." Over the next few years the dolls were made with 21 different

Above: *Cabbage Patch Kids dolls dominated the market in the first half of the 1980s. In 1986, for example, sales exceeded $1.2 billion.*

Right: *Cabbage Patch Kids dolls, protected by two Brinks guards, head for a drug-store in Illinois, where they will be auctioned at the rate of one an hour.*

Below: *An older fan of Cabbage Patch Kids dolls hugs three examples. Each came with adoption papers and birth certificate.*

Left: *The Liddle Doll Family, as produced by Mattel in the 1980s.*

Above: *One of the Middleton Doll Company's dolls, known as First Moments, Christening, from 1989.*

faces and many different hairstyles and outfits. Seven factories were making them in the United States, and four foreign producers were licensed, including Lili Ledi (Mexico), Jesmar (Spain), Triang Pedigree (South Africa), and Tsukuda (Japan). Their values on today's market vary according to availability, rareness, and the popularity of certain models. The variations among Cabbage Patch Kids dolls are larger than those among any other modern dolls.

During their first year on the market, Cabbage Patch Kids were available without dimples (#1); with two dimples, large eyes, and no freckles (#2); with one dimple and large eyes (#3); and with two dimples and a pacifier (#4). There were boys with a red shag hairdo, African-American dolls with freckles, Baldie dolls of both sexes without hair, girls with single and double ponytails, "poodle" haircuts, "popcorn" hairdos, single and double braids, and single teeth. Altogether, seven hair colors, five eye colors, and 13 basic hairstyles evolved – all with variations.

Named varieties of Cabbage Patch Kids include the Cornsilk Kids, Splash Kids, Preemies, Talking Kids, Babies, Twins, Travelers, Astronauts, Baseball Kids, Clowns, and Ringmasters. Among the foreign-made dolls, the most desirable include the Lili Ledi freckled dolls; the Jesmar dolls of 1983 with their well-placed eyes, freckles, and pacifiers; the Triang Pedigree dolls with their gaudy yellow hair and/or freckles and pacifier; and Tsukuda's 1983 models with red or lemon-colored hair and brown eyes, or with such specialty outfits as kimonos, baseball uniforms, and karate and samurai clothing. The Japanese powder-scented dolls are highly valued on the collector's market.

Vogue dolls remained popular into the 1980s, as the original Ginny dolls became increasingly valuable. The Little Imp doll originated by Arranbee was reprised in the 10½-inch (26.8-cm) Country Cousin, with freckles, straw hat, and sleep eyes. Steiff made a Ginny Pup, and many Ginny Exclusives were made between 1986 and 1991, including those for Shirley's Dollhouse, Gigi and Sherry Meyers, and Toy Village.

Ideal Toy and Novelty Company continued to manu-

facture dolls that were as popular with a new generation as Flossie Flirt had been in 1925. Hasbro introduced a wide-eyed Real Baby doll designed by Judith Turner in 1985. It was 20 inches (50.9 cm) long, with vinyl head and limbs and a cloth body, boxed with a life-size baby bottle. The doll had inset eyes with hair lashes and six different outfits, including a yellow sleeper, a pink-and-white bunny-ears suit, and a blue two-piece outfit with a hood. It was available in both an Awake and an Asleep model, as an African-American or Caucasian.

Another Hasbro innovation of the 1980s was the Fashion by Me doll – a 13-inch (33-cm) fashion doll with vinyl head, painted features, and rooted hair. The body was made from one piece of plastic, with high-heel feet. A soft vinyl-lining cutout along all sides to hold material enabled the child to dress the doll without sewing: "Just tuck into magic seams." It came with materials and patterns, shoes, stand, and handbags. Eight other clothing kits were also available.

Horsman maintained its reputation with new entries like Pudgie Baby, a 24-inch (61-cm) lifelike baby doll with a plastic body and vinyl head and limbs. The doll came with a short pink yoked smock and white bootees tied with pink ribbon. Novelty dolls like Horsman's Poor Pitiful Pearl, Hebee-Shebee, and Billikin, were acquired by collectors, along with such character dolls as the composition-and-cloth Jackie Coogan with painted eyes, dating from 1921.

An interesting footnote to the Madame Alexander story is the fact that Cissy-faced dolls were used to design costumes for the Ice Capades for many years. The dolls were taken on the road by the show's advance publicists, insured for hundreds of dollars, and displayed at the Ice Capades' California studio. The costumes created in miniature for these dolls are a wonder of sequins, feathers, ruffles, and rhinestones. Some of them have found their way to the collector's market, including "Rose Marie" (1949-50), "My Fair Lady" (1961-62), "Show Boat" (1956), and "Cole Porter" (1963).

Nancy Ann Storybook Dolls became increasingly popular with collectors, from the original painted bisque models of the 1940s to the later hard-plastic and vinyl versions. The only indication of the doll's identity is a paper tag around the wrist with the doll's name on it. The popular Muffie doll was reintroduced in hard plastic with jointed knees. "Month dolls," produced from 1941 on, were made of painted bisque, with unjointed hips and socket heads. June is an attractive example, with curly blonde hair and a rose-trimmed pink-and-white-lace gown. Collectable plastic Storybooks include Autumn, Sabbath, Princess Monon Minette, Queen of Hearts, Christening, and A Pretty Girl Is Like a Melody. Baby and African-American Nancy Ann dolls are increasingly rare.

Left: *Barbie conquers Eastern Europe as one little girl from East Germany buys a doll in a West German town shortly after the collapse of the Iron Curtain.*

Effanbee Limited Edition Club dolls of the recent past include Susan B. Anthony, Princess Diana, Sherlock Holmes, and Bubbles. Composition dolls of the American Children series, including Barbara Ann, designed by Dewees Cochran, have become increasingly valuable. The lovely Honey and Toni hard-plastic dolls of the 1950s are highly prized. The Champagne Lady doll, modeled on Alice Lon of television's "Lawrence Welk Show," is a fine example of a vinyl Effanbee doll of the 1950s.

Eegee dolls, originally marked "E.G.," from the initials of founder E.G. Goldberger, are now marked "Eegee" or "Goldberger." Recent dolls from this company include the 12-inch (30.5-cm) Dolly Parton, and the baby doll Bundle of Joy, with a cloth body and vinyl head and limbs. This doll harks back to the past in having painted features and molded hair. It is dressed like a newborn baby, and has a snub nose and closed, smiling mouth. Eegee is also well known for its celebrity dolls, including Prince Charles, all-vinyl and fully jointed, with painted brown hair and blue eyes. Made in Hong Kong, the doll is marked on the head "L.H.&H./© 1982," for the copyright holder Launey, Hachmann & Harris, Inc. A companion doll is Princess Diana, dressed in a replica of Princess Diana's wedding gown with a two-and-a-half-foot (76.2-cm) bridal train. The House of Nisbet has also produced several Princess Diana dolls, including a porcelain wedding-dress model in a limited edition of 3500.

Mattel Inc., the Fortune 500 toy company that produces Barbie, is headed at the time of writing by Jill Barad, who presides over the manufacture of more than a million Barbie dolls a week, representing a billion dollars' worth of revenue to Mattel in 1993. In an interview published in *People* magazine on May 9, 1994, Barad said, "I'm very conscious of showing that Barbie's been an astronaut, or that she's a doctor. It's what we do in the world, not what we look like, that will be remembered." Millions of little girls who have become women since the 35-year-old Barbie was introduced would probably agree, as they purchase Barbie dolls for *their* children.

As the twentieth century draws to a close, it is hard to predict what the age of microchips and new materials will mean to the future of doll-making and collecting. But is it safe to predict that these small images will retain their hold on our hearts and our imaginations as new generations of children take their place in the world.

Right: *A human Barbie lookalike poses with a selection of Mattel's most important creation.*

INDEX

ACKNOWLEDGMENTS

The author and publishers would like to thank Mike Rose for designing this book and Helen Dawson for compiling the index. Special thanks are due to Robin Langley Sommer, Nick Nicholson and Vina Cooke for their extensive help. The following individuals and agencies provided photographic material:

The Bettmann Archive, pages: 1, 42(bottom).
The Free Library of Philadelphia, page: 28.
Barbara Guyette, pages: 40(bottom), 44(top left), 49(bottom left), 60, 66, 72, 73(both), 74, 75(both), 76, 77(both), 78, 79, 80, 81, 82-83, 83(both), 84, 85, 88, 89, 91, 93, 96, 97(both), 98, 99(both), 100(both), 101, 102, 103, 104, 105(both), 106, 107, 108, 109, 111, 112, 114(both), 115, 116, 119, 120, 126-127, 127, 128, 129(both), 130, 132, 133, 137, 140, 141, 142, 148, 149, 152, 153.

Hasbro, Inc., pages: 118(G.I. Joe® is a registered trademark of Hasbro, Inc. All rights reserved).
Mattel, Inc., pages: 2-3, 9, 86-87, 87, 90, 94, 95(both), 122, 125 (Photos courtesy of Mattel. Barbie and associated names and Mattel, Inc., El Segundo, CA).
Nick Nicholson, pages: 6, 7(all three), 8(both), 10, 11, 12, 13(both), 14, 15(both), 16(both), 17, 18(both), 19, 20(both), 21, 22, 22-23, 24, 25, 26, 27(all three), 29(both), 30, 31(all three), 32(both), 33(both), 34, 35(all three), 36, 37, 39(both), 40(top), 41, 42(top), 43, 44(top right and bottom), 45, 46(bottom), 48, 49(top left and right), 50, 51, 52(both), 53, 54, 55, 56(both), 57, 58, 59, 61, 62(both), 63, 64(both), 65, 67, 68(both), 69, 70, 71, 117, 123, 136.
Reuters/Bettmann Newsphotos, pages: 144-145, 146, 146-147, 154, 156-157.
UPI/Bettmann, pages: 4-5, 38, 45(top), 47, 92, 110, 113, 124, 131, 134, 135, 138, 143, 150, 150-151.